UNDERSTANDING BODY TALK

UNDERSTANDING BODY TALK

(Original title: Your Silent Language)

By Elizabeth McGough
Illustrated by Tom Huffman

SCHOLASTIC BOOK SERVICES
New York Toronto London Auckland Sydney Tokyo

For Mark, Steve, and Mike.

This book is sold subject to the condition that it shall not be resold, lent, or otherwise circulated in any binding or cover other than that in which it is published — unless prior written permission has been obtained from the publisher — and without a similar condition, including this condition, being imposed on the subsequent purchaser.

Copyright © 1974 by Elizabeth McGough. This edition is published by Scholastic Book Services, a division of Scholastic Magazines, Inc., by arrangement with William Morrow & Company, Inc.

1st printing . . . . October 1975
Printed in the U.S.A.

Contents

1. What Message Do You Send?   8
2. Eye Movements   14
   What the Eyes Say / Eye Behavior in Public Places / A Dirty Look / Blinking / Clues to State of Mind
3. Facial Expressions and Head Movements   23
   Range of Expressions / Smiles and Other Mouth Gestures / Head Movements / Social Faces
4. Hands, Arms, and Legs   33
   Confidence and Doubt / Putting Up a Barrier Self-Control / Yes, No, Maybe / Male and Female
5. Postures   47
   Personality Expression / Defense and Aggression / Leadership / Inclusion or Exclusion
6. The Courting Game   63
   Typical Courting Gestures / The Qualifiers Courting Gestures in Other Situations
7. To Touch or Not to Touch   71
   Function of Skin / Skin Hunger / Handshakes and Tickling / Some Special Touches
8. Space Needs   86
   A Sense of Territory / Our Space Bubble Personalities / Space and Status
9. Body Language Spoken Here   100
   The Arabs / The Spanish / The English / The Germans / The French and the Austrians / The Japanese / Chileans and Other Cultures

Selected References   118

Introduction

There's language in her eye, her cheek, her lip,
Nay her foot speaks; her wanton spirits leak out
At every joint and motive of her body.
WILLIAM SHAKESPEARE

Imagine this scene. You and your friends are watching a crime thriller on television. A lawyer is ready to cross-examine a witness suspected of armed robbery. Just as the witness takes the stand, there is silence. A message flashes across the screen. "We regret the loss of the sound portion of our program. Please stay tuned."

The program continues in silence.

The witness looks straight at the lawyer, who is cross-examining him. You watch the lawyer speak as he walks slowly back and forth in front of the witness stand. The witness holds his head high; his hands are still. Then the witness puts his hand to his collar, as he begins to speak. The lawyer strides back and forth briskly, his hands now gesturing as he pursues his questions. The witness smooths his hair into place, again tugs at his collar. He looks away from the lawyer, looks toward the door as he speaks. The lawyer squares his shoulders as he stands in front of the witness, and he speaks to the accused. The witness looks down at the floor. His shoulders sag, and he slumps in his seat. Walking quickly, the lawyer crosses the courtroom in front of the witness, pausing for an instant in front of the judge. The witness stands; his hands grip the railing. He walks away, looking very tired, slumped over.

You and your friends start to talk about the program, hardly aware that you didn't actually hear what was going on. You know what happened. You might even talk about the thoughts and emotions of the lawyer and the witness. All of this information was communicated to you by the way these people moved in the situation. When you could not hear the words, you concentrated on what an eye movement, an arm gesture, a posture, or a man's walk could tell you. You "listened" to body language.

Scientists have been concerned with communications for thousands of years. But only in recent years have researchers been able to convince us that body movements are effective communication tools. In fact, a new science has been born in your generation, a science called *kinesics*. According to Dr. Ray L. Birdwhistell, inventor of this new science, "Kinesics is the systematic study of how human beings communicate through body movement and gestures."

When you walk into a room, you communicate with everyone there without saying a word. Faster than words, your body sends the message. What kind of feedback do you get from the group? By learning the language of body movement, we may discover what gestures to use to produce the reaction we want from the other person. We may also learn to react more quickly to others in their needs. Nonverbal clues account for many decisions we make.

Psychologists analyze message impact this way: 7 percent verbal (choice of words), 38 percent vocal (tone), and 55 percent body language. Can we afford to misread these messages?

To bring some order to this broad territory of language without words, I have chosen to begin with communication patterns, then eye, facial, and head movements, and entire body postures. I will also discuss other keys to our silent language, from space needs and courting gestures to cross-cultural differences.

CHAPTER ONE

What Message Do You Send?

You can stop talking, but you cannot stop "saying" something through the body idiom.
DR. ERVING GOFFMAN
Presentation of Self in Everyday Life

Did you ever have a simple conversation with your father, yet come away with the vague, uneasy feeling that he was in a bad mood? You told him how tough your science project was; he sympathized with you. You relayed a phone message for him. He acknowledged it. A very ordinary conversation. Yet you felt sure that he was angry about something.

Many of us call this feeling intuition. It's actually a skill, the ability to interpret nonverbal behavior. When two people meet, they communicate both in words and in body movements. Possibly you saw a scowl begin around your father's mouth, or his eyes were cold and his forehead lines hinted at anger. His body seemed tense. Any movement may have been sharp, sudden.

When we try to communicate, sometimes we get through and sometimes we do not. Many times our nonverbal language contradicts the spoken message. Feedback plays a powerful role in communication. We see how our message is received by watching an individual reaction. We can, if we are alert, learn whether our message is received positively or negatively. Sometimes we decide that we must change our approach if the feelings sent back to us are not what we hoped they would be.

Sue-Ellen would rather disappear into the woodwork than have all eyes on her. She hates to be noticed. When she arrives at a party, she is self-conscious. Her shoulders are hunched in. She looks away as quickly as possible, makes no eye contact with anyone in the room. She communicates unfriendliness, withdrawal, lack of desire for interaction with others. Her defensive way sets her apart from others.

If we enter a room the way Sue-Ellen does, without the customary polite nods and gestures of greeting, we shall probably get a cool response in return. When we look off into space or out over the crowd, either because we are shy or aloof, we create hostility. Our lack of greetings say that we consider ourselves superior, somehow better than others.

As Sue-Ellen did, we would no doubt spend the evening like a lonely wallflower. But we need not feel isolated, if we learn to develop our talent for better communications. Then we may see what messages we really send. We may be able to recognize how we put up barriers to friendships. We may also learn to read others more accurately.

In the past two decades scientists have made enormous strides in the study of communications. Dr. Birdwhistell, Senior Research Scientist at the Eastern Pennsylvania Psychiatric Institute, first reported on the *structured* nature of body-motion communication in his publication, *Introduction to Kinesics,* in 1952. Dr. Birdwhistell feels that "body motion and facial expression belong to a learned, coded system and that there is a 'language' of movement comparable to spoken language, both in its structure and in its contribution to a systematically ordered communicative system." He feels that all movements of the body have meaning, that none are accidental. Further, he claims that all significant body language is learned, not inherited.

Dr. Birdwhistell has devised a notational system to break down kinesics to their basics, or to their smallest recordable movement, called a *kine*. For example, open eyes are o o. Closed eyes, — —. A wink of the right eye becomes o —. A wink of the left eye, — o.

According to Dr. Jurgen Ruesch, in his book *Nonverbal Communication*, there are four communication settings:

1. Intrapersonal, or self-centered. The message begins and ends with the same person. These messages indicate our thinking and feeling.

2. Interpersonal system. Two people communicate.

3. Group system. Several or many people are involved. Each has a special position within the network of that group.

4. Societal system. So many persons are involved that individual identity is lost.

As small children, up to five years old, we communicate primarily with one person at a time. In later childhood, from six to twelve years old, group communication begins with several persons at a time, especially with children of our own age and sex. During adolescence, from twelve to eighteen, we make increased attempts to communicate with "out" groups. Adolescents choose to relate to a member of the opposite sex or to a slightly older person of the same sex. When we are about eighteen years old, we begin to relate well to persons of all ages, differing status, origins, and backgrounds. Perhaps this development explains the remark of a young adult who said, "Amazing how smart my father became between the time I was eighteen and the time I was twenty-five." The peak of group development is reached in adolescence. One half to two thirds of young people from eleven to seventeen years old belong to some kind of group.

Social scientists feel that we join groups to be a visible, active "somebody." One student commented, "Oblivion may be worse than infamy." He would rather be recognized or identified with something bad than not be recognized at all!

In addition to gestures, the way in which we dress says something about us. In the first instant that we see someone, we notice the "mask" he wears, the facade he presents to the world. Through careful discipline in our society, we present our personal appearance the way that is expected of us. Young adults conform to the standards of dress set in their peer group. Conformity is so important that some people will buy only the currently popular brand of clothing or shoes. One fourteen-year-old boy was horrified at the thought of buying anything but Converse basketball shoes. He said, "My friends will laugh at me if I buy these cheapies."

Comfortable jeans, long hair, and casual clothing are acceptable for most occasions in a teen-ager's life. In the business world, people wear neat clothes, keep their hair combed and their faces clean. Dr. Erving Goffman notes that at certain times of the day, in evening rush hours on the subway, for example, some of us allow a kind of righteous exhaustion to take over on our faces. When we are weary at the end of the day, we let our hair down. Usually, though, we do not let our face show exactly how we feel. We have a certain face for company, for parties, for business, and even for funerals.

Men take care to see that they are properly buttoned and zipped. Women sit carefully with their legs close together so they will not show their thighs. If we present ourself differently, in dress or in body posture, we show lack of regard for normal social behavior. We show, by our carelessness, that we sneer at others present or that we have little regard for the occasion. Suppose you are invited to a sorority tea. You show up in old faded jeans and hiking boots. Obviously you don't care and have no desire to be involved.

Opposite, though, is the young wife who puts on something pretty, combs her hair, and uses a favorite perfume before she greets her husband in the evening. He asks, "You look lovely. Are we expecting someone special?" She answers, "Yes, I'm expecting you." By her appearance, she says something nice.

With appearance and body movements, we send many silent messages. Our gestures sometimes contradict the spoken word. A politician spoke before an audience made up largely of students. He said, "I love the young people of this country," as he made karate chops with his fists on the speaker's stand. Few of us would accept his words as sincere.

Often, however, the spoken word is endorsed by the gestures that accompany it. For example, a mother comforts her small child with soothing words when he is hurt. As she makes soft sounds, she gently strokes his hair. Her gestures are in harmony, or are congruent, to use the language of kinesicists.

Yet not all body language is nearly as evident. Nor do single isolated gestures always convey the true meaning of a situation. In fact, many sociologists feel that we must look for the gesture cluster, or group of gestures. Each gesture is only one input. We should watch the prior and following gesture for accurate readings.

Each gesture can be countered or confused by another following movement. To be aware of the gesture cluster helps control our judgment. We should never leap to conclusions based on a single gesture. The whole situation, or context, of a happening must be considered. We all notice subtle changes in a person as he responds to us, to what we say or do. These communications take place simultaneously on different levels of consciousness, from our subconscious to full awareness.

Experts look for patterns in the whole situation to establish meaning for our gestures. Some anthropologists say that gestures are the forerunners of speech. Communicating with gestures began with the caveman, yet only recently has the significance of gestures been recognized. Considering all the efforts made toward better verbal communication, we may think that nonverbal messages are comparatively unimportant. It takes *both* to make clear communication in most cases. But probably more feelings, intentions, and emotions are communicated in nonverbal behavior than in all verbal ways put together.

CHAPTER TWO

Eye Movements

The eyes of men converse as much as their tongues.
RALPH WALDO EMERSON

Your eyes have a whole repertoire of signals — from eyes that meet and hold another's in defiance (as to a parent or teacher, testing their authority), to eyes that say "I find you interesting." Normal eye contacts last about one second before someone looks away. Without a word, David can cause almost any girl to say, "He makes me feel special. His eyes say it all."

If you want to tip a relationship to a slightly warmer one, when his eyes meet yours, try holding his gaze longer. This response is just a variation of old-fashioned flirting. But it works!

Our eyes tell many stories. We have all seen the eyes of two people in love. We have seen two angry people glare at each other. In each case, no words were needed to explain the emotions passing between those involved.

What the Eyes Say

Consider some of the feelings that eyes can convey. They can threaten, frighten, hate, love, seduce, ignore, plead, or reproach. They can be confident, depressed, guilty or forgiving.

They can also be shifty and evasive. Experts tell us that shifty eyes usually say the person has something to hide. Anthropologists who specialize in kinesic communication have demonstrated this fact in experiments in which people were coaxed to cheat on a test. A filmed study showed the cheaters were easy to spot. Minute eye tremors betrayed the misdeed. The person you feel uneasy around is often the one "who won't look you in the eye" when he talks. Store security forces admit they can often spot shoplifters from eye behavior. In our culture, honesty demands that we look someone in the eye.

The exception is the extremely shy person who avoids eye contact or minimizes it if at all possible. They may be sincere and honest, but their eyes unintentionally communicate doubt and possible lying. Researchers say that people have more eye contact while listening than when they talk.

According to studies done in England, you can tell whether a person is an introvert or an extrovert by watching his eyes while you're talking to him. Subjects were given personality tests. The personality type, introvert or extrovert, was established through these tests. They were then asked to discuss something with another subject for three minutes while a psychologist watched eye movements from a hidden observation post. Introverts met the gaze of the other person only at brief intervals, then looked away. Extroverts looked directly at the person they were talking to much of the time. They turned their eyes away only half as often as the introverts.

Eyes, too, act as traffic signals to control coversation time. When you talk, you pause briefly to organize your thoughts. You look at the listener with short glances from time to time to make sure he is still with you. You are watching for feedback. Sometimes you'll notice his attention wanders. His eyes and eyebrows tell you if he understands what you say. If he is attentive, his eyes tell you, "Okay, go on. I'm listening." A rather long glance from you signals that you are through talking. Now it's his turn to talk. Watch a couple of conversations sometimes, and see if this pattern isn't followed.

Eyebrows have a variety of signals in their more than twenty possible positions. A bilateral eyebrow raise (both brows shoot up at the same time) shows doubt or questioning, says, "Repeat the message, please." Or it says, "Are you sure of that?" Males talk more with their eyebrows than females do, according to Dr. Birdwhistell.

Eye Behavior in Public Places

Proper eye behavior on our streets in the United States calls for a delicate balance of attention and inattention. We are expected to look at a passerby only enough to show that we are aware that he is there. If we look too little, we are thought to be haughty; too much, and we are considered nosy, inquiring. Sociologist Dr. Erving Goffman, who studies behavior in public places, explains that we usually watch each other until we are about eight feet apart. Just as we reach the eight-foot distance, each person signals in which direction he will pass. We do so with a quick glance in that direction. Then both parties turn their eyes downward. Goffman describes this behavior as a "kind of dimming of lights." The passing goes smoothly most of the time. Occasionally, though, the signals get confused. Then something like a little dance takes place as each tries to let the other pass.

While looking down at the ground is acceptable street behavior, it is not a good idea in public speaking. To give an effective speech we are taught to make eye contact with our audience. The only way to have good eye contact is to look a person directly in the eye. Look right at the person, and when the glance is returned move on. Don't stare off in space or out over the tops of heads. Your eyes should not be fixed on your notes — or on the nearest exit door! Your audience won't really feel in touch with you unless you make your eyes behave properly.

The importance of eye contact for speakers was established by John Mills in 1961 in his doctoral thesis at the University of Southern California. He found that speakers rated "sincere" looked at their audience an average of 63.4 percent of the time they talked. Speakers rated "insincere" had eye contact only 20.8 percent of the time they spoke.

A youth employment service counselor offered this advice to a young person seeking a job. "If I could tell you only one thing," he said, "I'd tell you to look at the interviewer. Look directly at him. Make good eye contact."

Our eyes reveal many things about us. They tell when we see something we like. A pretty girl in a bikini will cause a man's pupils to dilate. If you play cards, watch out when your opponent's eyes light up and his pupils dilate. He probably has a real powerhouse.

Young adults use body language quite effectively when they roll their eyes. As her father says something she dislikes, Sharon rolls her eyes upward as if to say, "Oh no!" This movement is usually accompanied by other gestures. As they roll their eyes, young people sigh — or stifle a *tsk-tsk* sound. They close their lips, cock their heads, or stretch their neck upward. Parents get the message loud and clear. One parent claims this gesture is the most exasperating one her four teen-agers use. She says, "They even use it at the dinner table in response to each other."

Eyes sometimes say things we are reluctant to put into words. For example, a young girl gazed longingly at a beautiful expensive coat in a store window. Her mother glared. She gave the girl a cold look, jerked her arm to come away. Each understood what the other was not willing to say out loud.

A Dirty Look

We all know how it feels to get a "dirty look." A sixteen-year-old girl said, "Adults often give you a dirty look. They make you feel that you are just a little kid. Clerks do this in a store, when they wait on adults first even though you are there before them. They see you. But it's as though you aren't actually there." A boy that same age complained that adults give him the "You're not really there" treatment on a golf course. Scientists term this eye behavior the *nonperson treatment*.

Usually we acknowledge the presence of others sufficiently to show that we have seen them. But we don't lock glances. Then we quickly withdraw our attention to let them know we are not prying or curious. Dr. Goffman calls this response *civil inattention*. We say, in body English, "I know you're there, but I won't intrude upon your privacy."

When with nonpersons, however, we may stare at them as though they were objects. Or if we feel someone is not even worthy of a glance, let alone a stare, we act as though we do not see him. We scarcely acknowledge his presence at all. This treatment is sometimes given to waitresses and servants. Adults also give it to children. They may introduce everyone present, but ignore a child. Parents sometimes talk about children in their presence acting as if they were not there. A mother may say, "Johnny was a born pessimist. He was a sourpuss even as a baby." By her body language, endorsed by the spoken word, this parent truly makes the child feel like a nonperson.

A friend told this story: "Once on the golf course I got ready to tee up my ball. I was playing with my husband and teen-age son, both excellent golfers. They stood close by, talked loudly, and acted as though they could not see me. By their lack of proper eye gestures, they indicated that they considered me, as a golfer, of little consequence."

Blinking

One of the most annoying of all gestures is the constant blinking of eyes. While blinking is considered a relief mechanism for the person who blinks, it arouses a wide range of emotions in others who see it.

The reactions vary from acute embarrassment for the individual (as when we are uncomfortable for someone who cannot control this mannerism) to annoyance and anger.

Brian, thirteen years old, cannot seem to control his blinking. Frustrated and annoyed, his mother says, "For heaven's sake, stop that."

An older brother says, "Brian, you drive me nutty with that blinking. I'm going to call you Blinky in front of your friends."

Both attacks on Brian compound his problem. For some reason, nervous or anxious children, particularly in early adolescence, do blink a great deal. When self-image is down, the lack of self-confidence is revealed in many ways. Clinical psychiatrist, Sandor S. Feldman, M.D., feels that chronic blinking in children is often an escape from being looked at by others. Anger or increased tension causes the rate of blinking to increase.

Dr. Feldman says young adolescents also use blinking to test a friend's courage. In his book, *Mannerisms of Speech and Gestures in Everyday Life,* he tells about a game played by a group of boys. One boy asks another seriously, "Do you have courage or not?"

"I have courage."

"Let me see. Were you in the forest?"

"Yes."

"Did you see a wolf?"

"Yes."

"Were you afraid?"

"NO!"

The friend stretches out his arm and waves it in front of the other boy's eyes. If his eyes blink, he is a liar and blinking proves that he is a coward. It implies, too, that if the boy were a man, he could control himself from blinking.

Blinking by a woman is a well-known come-hither signal. It invites a man to come closer. Or winking at each other shuts out others and says, "This is a private matter."

Clues to State of Mind

A psychiatrist who has done extensive kinesic research feels that there is a phase between the time we are consciously aware of our inner needs until we can take action. During that phase, we resort to restless and inhibited movements that go along with our unrelieved tension.

For example, his patient had to urinate and was too embarrassed to say anything about his discomfort. Eye movements and foot shuffling increased under increased bladder pressure. The patient needed to escape. He glanced toward the door repeatedly with fleeting eye movements. His restless feet seemed beyond his control. His kinesic behavior was subconscious. Through his body language he sent a message he could not yet put into words.

According to Dr. Feldman and other kinesicists, looking and seeing are two entirely different matters. Looking is a psychologically active step. It is "spying." Seeing is a psychologically passive step, "taking it in." For example, Ann comes to the party in a slinky halter dress. She walks over to Steve. She will be hurt if he doesn't see what she wants him to see. But he must not look. That would be spying, and she would be forced to move away from him. She must then consider him something less than a gentleman. A young man may *see* his mother or sister in a filmy nightgown. But he doesn't *look* or spy, in such a way as to make them feel they are wearing something sheer.

Some kinesic researchers have shown interest in one other function of our eyes, that of crying. Tears are wet and warm. In the chronic cryer or one who cries too easily, tears suggest a regression to intrauterine life (life in the uterus). Tears and amniotic fluid have a remarkably similar content of sugar, protein, and sodium chloride.

A body movement may have very little importance in one context, yet be extremely significant in another. The scowl we make when we slightly narrow our eyes and crease the skin between our brows may simply mark a point in conversation. But in another situation, we could be annoyed or deep in thought. If we focus on the facial expression alone, we won't get the exact meaning of a scowl. We need to know what the person says or does when he makes this gesture.

As we begin to see the patterns of our nonverbal language, we become more aware of the complex messages we send. We realize that our spoken words are but a fraction of what we communicate.

CHAPTER THREE

Facial Expressions and Head Movements

Everyone is a moon, and has a dark side which he never shows to anybody.
MARK TWAIN

Can you tell how someone feels about you by reading body language? Authorities claim you can, from the look of scorn, however fleeting, to the subtle nods and bright eyes that say someone is receptive to your thoughts.

Katie, seventeen, says, "My friend's mother doesn't like me. I know she doesn't." I asked Katie why she thought this. "Well, for one thing, she doesn't look at me when I talk to her," Katie explained. "She looks away toward the door or across the room, as though she wants to escape. And sometimes she looks at me as if to say, 'You look funny in those clothes.' I guess it's the way her eyes look cold and her lips are pressed together. She doesn't need to say one negative word to me." The mother's body language had sent a message loud and clear.

Imagine a look of mockery on your own face. Teeth come together, lips close with a slight downward turn. Usually we are quick to erase such a look from our face before others see our inner thoughts. If you are observant, though, you may learn to catch all the meaning behind the mask people wear — or think they wear. As you become more in tune with body communications, you will know when to give your friends or your parents a wide berth. You will spot the times people are tense. You will also begin to understand your own body language, to be aware of what messages *you* send.

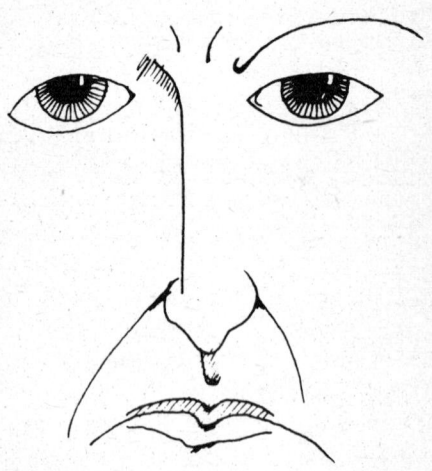

Range of Expressions

Our facial expressions are our most readily observed body language. In filmed studies of facial expressions researchers have focused on specific parts of the face, from furrowed brows to the mouth and chin. One team of researchers in England catalogued eighty face and head gestures. In spite of the number of possible facial expressions, this area of body language is the one in which scientists find the most universal agreement on what each motion means.

Let's think about facial expressions. We can easily recall many ways we use our face to send a message. For displeasure, we frown, stick out our tongue.

As Dr. Birdwhistell explains, "If an emotional disturbance occurs within an individual, it is highly likely that some statement about this disturbance will be entered into the communication stream."

When something is said to make us aggressive or hostile, we rally to the occasion with immediate defenses. Our "emotional disturbance" flashes quickly into our appearance. We become tight-lipped. Our eyes narrow; our jaws tighten. We might stick out a defiant chin, much like a small boy rebelling against his parents. When we become defensive, we also arouse the defense level in the original speaker. As both parties become more irritated, we are less and less able to see each other's motives clearly. Communications completely fall apart, and we feel no one understands us.

Although many people communicate through facial expressions, few of us understand specifically how we do so. We've all heard the expression *poker face*. But what makes a poker face? Does the face have a blank look, no emotions showing, and are the pupils of our eyes in a moderate position?

From the beginning of recorded history, man's actions have been influenced by his interpretation of the expression on a person's face. Many ordinary kinds of behavior, such as biting our lip, wrinkling our forehead, are taken as words by people who see them. These statements are not intended for someone else. Yet they are still stated. Furthermore, they help others understand how we feel more accurately than words alone, especially if the person knows us. Some acts are not meant to communicate a message, such as nail biting, knuckle cracking, or fidgeting. They are interpreted by others, though, who assume things about the personalities of people who do them. You might recall meeting a friend's handsome older brother. Did you notice that he was chewing on a fingernail? That action said something to you, didn't it? You probably told yourself something like, "Hmm, he's not so poised after all."

Smiles and Other Mouth Gestures

A smile, or facial movement that looks like a smile, appears in circumstances accompanied by mounting tension, according to Dr. René Spitz. Dr. Spitz has studied smiles in tiny babies. He says, "Grandmothers used to say "When newborns smile, they have a bellyache,"" and he feels there is truth in this observation.

The facial movement of smiling appears to be present from birth. A smile movement has been filmed in a three-day-old infant. But not until our third month of life does the smiling response come as a result of specific stimulus. Scientists feel that a baby under one month old rarely, if ever, smiles in times an adult would find pleasant.

British researchers who studied facial gestures have identified and film-recorded nine different smiles. Three of them are common smiles: the simple smile, the upper smile, and the broad smile.

When we smile a simple smile, our lips are lightly together, no teeth show. We are usually by ourselves and not involved with anyone else. We are happy. The upper smile is defined as when only the upper teeth show. It is often a smile of greeting, as in "how do you do" smiles, with some eye contact. In the broad smile, we show both upper and lower teeth. We are laughing, and eye-to-eye contact is not usual-

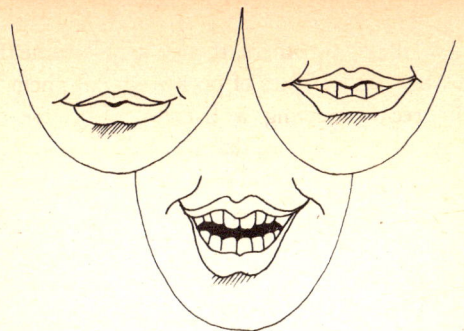

ly seen. The laughing smile is frequently seen during play, when we are having fun.

Bret Harte once wrote, "He smiled a kind of sickly smile." These smiles are often seen by the keen observer. Many smiles are not associated with happy occasions. A weak smile is sometimes an apology for being forced to sit next to someone. Some smiles have only slight significance. The are merely part of the mask we wear. They do not show our inner emotions at all, such as when we must smile in greeting a neighbor or the mailman.

Most of us have seen the oblong, or polite, smile. This smile has no depth to it, although upper and lower teeth show. We may recall disliking the person who flashed this toothy grin at us. This smile conveys condescension to some of us, as when an old friend of the family greets us too heartily. One researcher comments, "Beware of the oblong smile." We use it when we feel we must be polite, as when we pretend to enjoy an off-color joke or the open attentions of someone we actually find repulsive.

Have you ever seen the "lip-in smile" on a bashful girl? It is similar to the upper smile, except that the lower lip is drawn in toward the teeth. Experts say this smile shows the person feels inferior to the person she is greeting or is with.

Cartoonists know how to draw mouth lines to convey various expressions. For a tight-lipped person, they draw a straight line. For a good-natured person, they tilt the mouth up at the corners. For contempt, the mouth is drawn turned down. To show inferiority feelings, the artist lifts the mouth at one corner and pulls it to the side. You may see this expression in a comic strip.

When our chewing muscles are habitually contracted, we look like a fighter, a tough. When muscles are used excessively as with foreheads that wrinkle constantly, they remain semicontracted. They then mark the personality structure of that person. Try doing this exercise. Pretend you are chewing a large caramel. Hold your teeth in that position for a minute. Look in the mirror. Do you look ready for a fight? Now wrinkle your forehead and frown. Do you look worried? Have you ever seen someone who looks perpetually worried?

Some mouth gestures are common only to men. Spitting is one of these. Boys like to have spitting contests to show that they are men. For some reason, spitting is a sign of aggression and virility. It also shows contempt or disgust. Men like to spit from a high bridge into a lake to watch ripples form. Adolescent boys spit when they are in company of other boys.

Head Movements

In a National Institute of Health study, Dr. Richard Renneker found that using a large number of speech-accompanying gestures or inappropriate ones often causes miscommunication rather than a clear message. In films studied, eye-area movements were first in frequency, head movements second, and other speech-accompanying gestures, third. Too many gestures act as "noise." They distract from the verbal message.

In a high-school speech class, one student with a booming voice gave an informative speech on "How to Enjoy a Horse Race." He paced back and forth in his enthusiasm. His arms pounded wildly like hoofbeats as he described that ton of horse flesh thundering around the track. His eyes flashed. His face turned from side to side rapidly as he gestured toward the scene he was enthusiastically creating. Soon the audience lost track of the information being given. He had distracted them with his facial and body movements. His gestures became "noise." A typical comment on the speech was, "Fun to watch, but I don't know a thing about a horse race."

We are often not aware of the gestures we make. Many times a negative head gesture accompanies a positive statement. A person says, "It was absolutely fantastic," as he shakes his head from side to side. Can you visualize someone relating a sight he considered almost unbelievably beautiful or terrible? He probably is using the "negative kind of motion with a positive exclamation," said as if to deny that such a thing could truly happen or exist.

We also see people who unconsciously shake their heads back and forth when they disapprove of something. Once in church I saw a noticeable example of this gesture. Tom was a very outspoken critic of plans to build a new church. As the pastor spoke about the need for the new church, Tom crossed his arms and shook his head from side to side — totally unaware that he was doing so.

Negative head gestures have been observed in infants during the first three months of life. In fact, negative gestures predominate then, according to Dr. Ruesch. A baby throws his head back or pushes the mother's hands away from him. He can scream to prevent feeding. A baby's tongue may push the bottle away from his mouth. Positive motions, such as glowing eyes and babbling, increase in the third month of life.

We see many expressive movements of the head. An erect head shows stamina, pride, and strength, while a bowed head seems to convey humility, resignation, or guilt. We see people who sometimes duck their heads to one side. We also see a female turn her head aside close to one shoulder in a motion that seems to say, "I know I'm irresistible. Don't touch me."

Once during sidwalk interviews I talked with a young girl about teen volunteer work. She answered some questions and ended with a statement, "Well, I like it, that's all." Then she abruptly cocked her head. Her gesture, along with her facial expression, said, "So there now. Don't bug me!" However, in other circumstances, head cocking is a provocative gesture that females use to show they are interested in you.

We lift our head as if to seek divine guidance. If you see someone look up at the ceiling while you are talking, however, they are probably bored. Do you recall sitting with your head back, eyes staring at the ceiling, when you had tuned someone out?

We also communicate with our head if we do not look *up* when someone tries to talk with us. In this way we block communications.

Carla wants to talk to her father, but he is reading the paper. Carla sits down in a chair near him. She says, "I'm not going to the basketball game Friday night with Steve."

Dad keeps on reading, maybe says, "Umm."

"Have you got a minute, Dad?" Carla asks.

"Sure." Dad looks up slightly for an instant, then continues reading.

His inattentiveness says, "I haven't time or real interest." Carla walks away, hurt.

Social Faces

Dr. Goffman has done some interesting studies on the many faces we wear. One of them was conducted on Shetland Isle. There, when a neighbor or visitor came to visit, he was expected to wear at least a hint of a warm smile as he entered the cottage. Since there were no obstructions outside the cottage and little light within, the visitor could be observed without his knowledge as he approached the cottage. Islanders found great pleasure in watching the guest drop whatever expression he had, then pick up a sociable one as he reached the door. Some islanders got wise to the game and began to adopt a social face a long way from the house.

Think about your expression the next time you walk to the door of someone's house. Do you put on a happy face as you get near the door? Have you seen others getting ready for social interaction as they come toward a group of people?

Mark Twain once said, "Man is the only animal that blushes. Or needs to." We often see this facial reaction in group behavior when somebody goofs. How does the offender save face? Dr. Goffman tells about several ways a person may act when he finds himself "out of face" or embarrassed. He can pretend that nothing happened, make a joke of it, or he can be acutely shamefaced and apologetic. During the brief moment while he decides which tactic to follow, others unconsciously protect him by looking away. This behavior gives him time to think of a way to save face.

For example, Brian joins Karen, Sue, and Bob in a booth at the pizza parlor. Conversation centers around going-steady habits at school. "You know what I think of anybody who wears matching T-shirts with his girl?" Brian quips. "That has to be the weirdest..." A body-language signal from Karen, perhaps a facial expression or a kick under the table, stops him cold. Sue and Bob look at each other. Their slightly open jackets show matching T-shirts. Brian gets the message. He swallows and pulls at his collar (a feeling-cornered gesture). He begins, "Well, what I meant was..." Probably everyone has a good laugh, depending on Brian's cool.

If we bring our understanding of nonverbal behavior to a conscious level, we may find more accurate meaning in the messages we receive. While we may not become experts, this knowledge can help us to evaluate better before we react to an input.

CHAPTER FOUR

Hands, Arms, and Legs

He winketh with his eyes, he speaketh with his feet, he teacheth with his fingers.
PROVERBS 6:13-14

Although many of us can control our facial expressions rather well, few of us are aware of the hidden messages sent by our hands, arms, and legs. Stress and anxiety slip out from our hidden thoughts in spite of facial control.

Our expressive signs can qualify everything we say. Jean might say, "Of course I'm still going with Rick!" As she speaks, she slides his class ring off and on her finger. This gesture possibly means that she is thinking, "Should I break off with him and find someone else?" The experts tell us that when a woman opens and shuts her handbag repeatedly, she is also making a yes-no gesture.

Confidence and Doubt

Our hands give many clues to what we are thinking. Have you ever seen someone "steepling"? Imagine a panel discussion in which people sit at a table in front of you. While one person talks, as another waits her turn, she makes her hands form a church steeple with fingertips placed together. This person is either quite confident of what she plans to say, is smug, or she is proud and egotistical. You might be able to distinguish which category she falls into from other accompanying body language. Women generally use a rather subtle steepling, a more covert form. They put their hands in their laps and join fingers at about belt level. Some experts say the higher the steeple, the more important we feel. This gesture is one we commonly see when a minister delivers a sermon, pontificating to his flock.

If you're playing cards and someone steeples his cards under a fist, be wary. He likely has a strong hand against you.

When we touch or rub our nose with our index finger, we send an often-spotted qualifer of the spoken word. Dr. Birdwhistell tells of the time he asked a student at the University of Louisville how he liked a modern classic book. The student said he liked it very much, as he rubbed his nose. "The truth is," said Birdwhistell, "you don't like the book." The boy felt trapped. He admitted he found the book dull. He didn't know how he had given himself away.

The nose-touching gesture says, quite bluntly, "This stinks." At the very least, it is a negative reaction to the spoken word, unless you happen to have an itchy nose!

In fact, researcher Ruesch says, "It may not be an exaggeration to say that knowing everything about

the expressive movement of human hands and fingers would mean knowing everything about the origin and development of man as an individual and as a social being."

Some people play with their own hair or with a child's or a loved one's hair. Some people like to squeeze pimples. Their mouths actually water while pinching and squeezing blemishes. A similar sensation is described by people who like to wash each other's hair and massage the scalp. Such skin care actually invades a person's sensual territory, some experts say.

These activities were observed in a study of apes. Researchers found two primary instincts functioning: "to cling to" or "to go from" a mother. Many psychiatrists agree that when we touch the hair and face in periods of tension, the movements indicate regression to the instinct of clinging and going. These gestures are thought to express a situation in which having clung to our mother, we are then forced to leave her. Do you sometimes see a child, very tired, who twines a strand of hair around a finger and then brings it to her mouth?

Hand-to-mouth gestures have been the subject of much kinesic research. Suppose you share a secret with your brother about a surprise planned for your mother. Somehow you blurt out information about the surprise. Suddenly your hand goes to your mouth, as if to say, "Oops, I'm sorry." Or imagine that you are being questioned about something you'd rather not reveal. "Well, I didn't know you'd care," you might begin hesitantly. Chances are, your hand will come to rest somewhere near your mouth, perhaps to one side of your lips. These gestures happen when we'd rather not talk. We have said something we shouldn't have. We also see this gesture in times of astonishment.

Law-enforcement officers agree that this gesture communicates a wide range of emotions, from self-doubt to lying. A confident person speaks without hand-to-mouth gestures. He has no desire to cover his mouth as if to apologize for his conversation.

Can you picture someone sitting at a desk, a teacher or yourself, with elbows on the table, pyramid style, and hands cupped around his mouth? Some students of nonverbal behavior would say this person is playing cat and mouse. He is not ready to open up and reveal all the facts.

If we are enthusiastic and confident about what we are saying, we usually point and thrust our hands away from our mouth. If you watch for these qualifying gestures from others, you may get the message more clearly than if you only hear the spoken word.

Students have certain ways of raising their hand in a classroom. Sometimes the hand goes up haltingly, as if they are unsure. Students also learn how to make the teacher think the hand has been raised a long, long time.

Our hands and fingers seem especially capable of revealing our inner feelings. If you say to your little brother, "Look here, Billy," as you make a jabbing motion, you ruffle his feathers immediately. He knows you are scolding. Your gesture arouses his defenses and confounds any hope of getting cooperation from him. A pointing index finger says, "You're guilty." Have you ever heard the expression, *put the finger on him*? *Fingering* someone means that we have pointed out or identified a guilty person.

When we rub beside our ear or rub our eyes with our fingers, we communicate doubt. We say in nonverbal language, "Well, I don't know about that." If your father uses these movements, when you've asked for a favor, be sure that his resistance is up. You'll have to find a way to remove it before you can convince him. These gestures are similar to nose touching, which says something negative. Even a trained speaker will sometimes lay an index finger along the side of his nose, or he lightly touches the tip of his nose and upper lip. He may do so when he is not sure how the audience will react to what he is saying. He may not know how to approach a tough subject. When a person's nose is actually itchy, he scratches it more vigorously.

Another sign of doubt is nose pinching. A student trained in communications said, "When my dad pinches the bridge of his nose, I know that he is deep in thought. I just give him a little time to say what's on his mind."

Sometimes we have embarrassed hands or hands that pick at fingernails or scratch and pull at hair. Our embarrassed hands are thought to stem from traumatic experiences in our mother-child relationships.

Most kids say the person they have greatest trouble lying to is their mother. Women seem to have greater insight into children and their needs. One gave a typical example: "When kids lie," she said, "they go through a wide range of movements. Many of them are made with their hands. They clear their throat, blink more often, bring their hand to the back of the neck. They rub their nose or put their hands around their mouth, and sometimes they shrug their shoulders." The shoulder shrug shows they would like to get rid of something annoying.

Putting Up a Barrier

We complicate our interactions with other people by not being aware of our own body gestures. One student of kinesics told this story: "At a conference I sat next to a young writer. She began to tell me all the things wrong with the news media. I thought she made broad, sweeping statements and that she said unfair things. Although I tried to listen, I had folded my arms high on my chest. I felt quite stubbonly that she didn't know what she was talking about. When I realized what was happening, that I had turned off to whatever she said, I tried a different approach. I stopped judging, being so critical. I uncrossed my arms. Now I could listen more clearly. I began to understand and appreciate what she said, even though I did not agree."

We often see others pose in this closed-mind gesture, a defensive posture. Instead of changing course, we continue talking a blue streak. If we could recognize their body language, we would seek another way of getting our message across.

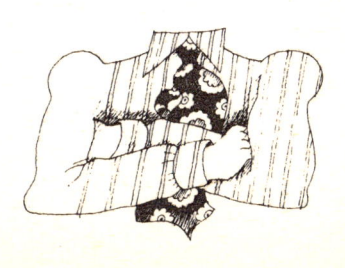

Even these familiar gestures are worth second notice, especially as we begin to reach out in jobs, in school, and in wider social relationships. You may recall gestures that annoy you, make you feel inferior. Do you recall a conversation with a teacher who appeared to give you a strict lecture, even though he didn't say anything harsh? Probably he crossed his arms on his chest or pointed a finger at you as he spoke. He sent a total message, not merely a verbal one. If you work with small children in any way, you might put this knowledge to practical use by avoiding these negative gestures in your own body language.

Self-Control

From tapping fingers to shuffling feet, your body can contradict what you say. A woman who shuffles her foot in and out of a shoe under the table is usually relaxed. Opposite though, is a man's foot that shuffles and taps. He signals anger or impatience, depending on the situation.

A female foot that swings in a back-and-forth motion indicates a bored woman. She is impatient for a conversation to be over or for some appointment to begin. Female legs have swinging, dangling gesture patterns that are provocative. Some legs say "not available to you" as they twist tightly together.

Gestures with our hands and feet often relate to self-control. We clench our fists in times of stress. Have you ever seen a man pace the floor with his arms behind his back, one hand gripping the other wrist? If you see someone in this pose, tread softly. He is worried. Tightly clenched hands also block communications. In fact, Charles Darwin observed that when a man uses this hostile gesture, he can cause another person to also clench his fists.

We try to keep our cool in a tense moment when we lock our ankles together. Think of a time when you sat in your counselor's office for an appointment about slipping grades. Did you clench your hands or lock your ankles? Airline stewardesses say they can spot worried travelers by watching for this posture.

Some people say that sitting with locked ankles

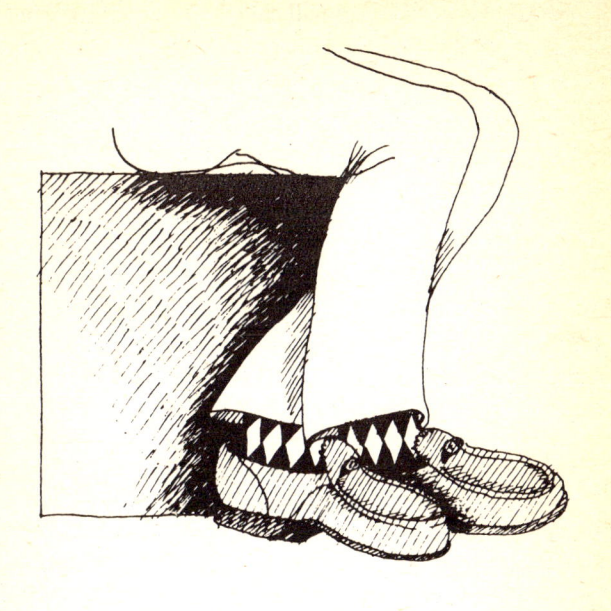

makes them feel more comfortable. The next time you find yourself sitting this way, unlock your ankles to see if you won't relax more. One interviewer for a large corporation said he could always tell when a job candidate was unsure of himself. He sat with tightly locked ankles!

When we are confident, self-control comes more easily. The reverse is also true. Our attitudes creep out in our behavior. When our self-image is down, we become nervous, unsteady, or frustrated. Our self-control falls apart. Our hands, arms, feet, and legs begin to tattle on our inner conflicts.

Yes, No, Maybe

When fingers drum on a table with monotonous rhythm, or feet tap with repetitious sounds, people are bored with what you say. When you see these signs as you talk, you should change your direction. Find a quick anecdote or story to perk them up, or you will continue to bore your listeners. When you see heads resting in hands, palm against the side of the face and droopy eyes, this pose also shows boredom.

We could all be more aware of body language that tells us how others react to us. When you "hear" something that disturbs you, be completely open about the problem. Say, "Have I somehow offended you?" Or, "I can see that you disagree. Let's talk about it." Your listener may be startled at first. But communications will surely improve.

Have you ever seen someone under fire tug at his collar? Did you get the impression that he felt cornered? Although this gesture is sometimes innocently made in a room that's stuffy, the "heat" of excitement is more likely the cause. When you are in heavy traffic, you may see a driver tug at his collar when a car cuts in front of him. He feels "hot under the collar." He may also use a hand-to-the-back-of-the-neck movement. This one is called a "defensive beating gesture." It's the same thing as verbally saying, "This gives me a pain in the neck." Women use this gesture with a slight variation. They move their hand into their hair, as if to say, "He sure gets in my hair." Or they may rub the back of their neck lightly with their fingers.

I recently saw Barbara Walters of the *Today Show* make the "pain-in-the-neck" gesture during a difficult television interview. Her subject evaded the questions and constantly interrupted Ms. Walters, an experienced interviewer.

People under stress also use a wipe-the-sweat-from-your-hands gesture. Boys wipe their hands on their pants leg, while girls may also wipe their hands on their jeans. When you see someone wring his hands or wipe sweat from them, there's trouble brewing inside. Attempt to help them relax before you begin serious talk. Try leaning toward this person.

We cross our fingers for good luck, a throwback to a more primitive time when people crossed their fingers to ward off evil spirits. We cross our fingers as if to say, "I'm not sure. I hope I'm right." We make a peace sign by holding the first two fingers in the form of a *V*. This was used by Winston Churchill as a *V* for Victory sign in World War II.

Hands show quite positive gestures, too. Have you ever seen a small boy rub his hands together as his mother takes a tray of cookies from the oven? This movement says, "Oh, boy, something good is on the way." We see this gesture in a meeting when someone expects to hear pleasant news, perhaps his name announced to receive some award. In a business meeting, you might see someone rub her hands as people gather around a conference table. What do you suppose she has in mind? Kinesic experts say she expects something good.

We use our hands to make evaluating gestures. We are not always aware of the inner feelings that say we are weighing, judging. The pose of the famous sculpture by Rodin, *The Thinker,* is a common evaluation gesture. You might see an old man people-watching from a park bench. He ponders what he sees, stroking his chin, as the parade of life goes by. A posture we should watch for is one with the fingers on chin, thumb under the chin, as the index finger points along the cheek. This person is critical, perhaps cynical. As we see others evaluate us, we become defensive of our position. Rather than bristling, we should look for a way to soften their attitude.

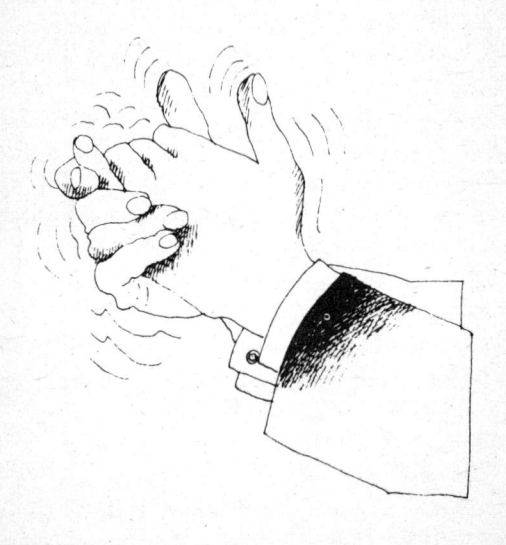

Male and Female

Females use their hands differently from the way males do. Jenny tried to convince her parents to let her go on an unchaperoned ski weekend. "Honestly," she said, as she slowly fingered her love beads, "we won't have any problems." Her hand movement signals that she doesn't quite believe what she has just said. Any female hand moving slowly to the throat area sends this message. People who know each other well often pick up messages very quickly out of awareness. Jenny's parents would probably sense her dilemma.

The female who lightly, and habitually, touches and strokes her breasts, sends the message, "I am truly lonely," even though she may wear the sexiest-looking dress at the party.

Women bring their hand to their chest in shock or surprise as they are told something horrible. Boys or men make hand-to-chest gestures, as they say, "I really mean it." They are showing loyalty or honesty. Can you picture a boy with both palms flat on his chest or with one palm to his chest and the other hand outstretched? These gestures date back to at least the Roman centurions. The centurion greeted his friend this way to show that he held no weapon.

Children raise one hand and show an open palm as they take oaths. "I swear to God," they assure their friends. You often see these gestures in more subtle form. If you are watchful, you will catch all the meaning intended in a conversation. You'll notice when gestures reinforce what is said or when they contradict the spoken word.

With a little effort, you can profit by some of the things scientists have learned about kinesics. For example, when you are interviewed for a job, if you assume an elaborately nonchalant position during the interview, arm thrown around the back of the chair, you have all but struck out. An employer doesn't want an unconcerned employee. Your nonchalance may be a cover for being uptight. But it may come across in body language as "I don't care."

Arms and legs send messages about us and about what we feel. A female sits with her leg tucked up under her to show that she is comfortable with this person. She may stand with arms akimbo in a self-satisfied pose. In this way she displays her breasts to advantage also. We stretch our arms forward to invite or comfort someone. One scientist considers this movement an almost universal gesture of peace. When we hold our hands out, palms open as we talk, we send an invitation to come to terms on something, even if only to consider our position.

Who could mistake the disgust as a man kicks the tire of a car. A boy sometimes kicks a stone in the road this way. A man may place a foot on an open desk drawer or his foot on a desk to show dominance or ownership. Men typically use this gesture. They also drape a leg over a chair to show their territorial rights. A young man might lean on his car, his arm stretched across the hood, in a pose that says unmistakably, "This is mine."

Some of our gestures with our limbs are deliberate, as when we cross our arms. Yet others are quite unconscious, as in nose touching and hand-to-mouth mannerisms. Our communications are like a giant puzzle. Each new facet of body language reveals something of how the puzzle fits together.

CHAPTER FIVE

Postures

*There's a kind of walk you walk
 when the world's undone you...*
"Walking Happy"
SAMMY CAHN, JAMES VAN HEUSEN

As the song says, even though we may try to conceal our feelings and emotions, our walk gives us away. At the University of Southern California, Dr. René Gailliet did extensive clinical studies of the way we walk. When we feel good and are in a happy mood, we thrust our body forward as we walk. Our step has a decided spring to it. If we are facing an emotional crisis and feel depressed, we slouch and walk flat-footed with no spring.

Chances are, when your father comes home from work at night, his initial greeting tells your mother what kind of an evening is in store. His words may be routine, "Hi, how was your day?" But the way he walks in the door, hangs up his coat, and falls into his chair may tell you more clearly than any words whether he is approachable or not. The subtle postures of fatigue, from shoulder droop to flat-footed walk, say, "I've had it today. Don't bug me about anything tonight." Or a relaxed yet aggressive stride, a springy step, and firm muscle tone show a mood of triumph. "It's been a good day. Let's do something fun tonight." Our body language says many things about our attitude toward ourselves and those around us. If we fully tune in to these communications, we may recognize when others should be left alone. Or we may see when an opportune time comes to ask a favor.

Personality Expression

A boy with a proud, firm walk strides into the room. His aggressive movements give the impression that he expects to lead the action, although he may not say so in words. A meek, apologetic boy with a shuffling walk makes people think that he expects to follow the lead of others.

Each of us has a distinct walk, recognizable to our friends. Some characteristics of our walk are due to body structure, our height and weight. But our walk varies with our mood. Posture, pace, and length of stride appear to be related to our emotions. We would all recognize when a friend is dejected if we see him walking head down, hands in pocket, shuffling along. When we see someone with a free-swinging stride, we think this person knows where she is going, has a goal clearly in mind.

Can you imagine an old Irish priest shuffling along, belly protruding, the keeper of his flock? His walk shows self-content. Other people have a tiptoeing gait, so quiet that no one hears them. This person is an exhibitionist at heart, although he tries to suppress these traits. We also recognize the cock-of-the-walk posture in a boy whose feet point outward, as his pelvic area thrusts forward in his stride.

Females communicate many things by the special ways they walk. An attractive female alone on a city street leaves no doubt by her fast walk that she is not a streetwalker looking for a pickup. One advertising manager described a familiar sight on the fashion pages — the model with wide stance, arms and legs akimbo, called the *pelvic thrust* — as a come-hither look. A girl who develops an intriguing hip-swinging walk knows that she will get attention and interest from the opposite sex.

Body signs can send information about how we feel about ourselves, what we think of others and of the setting. Did you ever notice someone who is really upset or uptight? Why did you think so? Researchers feel that we need to see a group of gestures put together to make this assumption. For example, your brother strides into the room, paces the floor, doesn't sit down right away. You suggest he sit down. Then he takes a chair far away from others. He abruptly crosses his arms and legs, looks out the window. You ask if everything is all right. He shifts his weight, points his feet or body toward the door. The message is clear. He is terribly worried. Someone else asks if everything is okay. Your brother may shout, "Get off my back. Leave me alone, will you?" Or he may just walk out.

No body posture by itself has a precise meaning, scientists are quick to warn. Body language and spoken language depend on each other. If you listen only to one and not the other, you will receive a distorted message.

As Dr. Goffman explains, "You can stop talking, but you cannot stop saying something through the body idiom. You either say the right thing or the wrong thing. You cannot say nothing. Usually we fit in or use the motions expected of us in a given situation. We all know something about the vocabulary of body symbols."

It's easy to pick out the pulled-in, hunched-over gestures of a shy, insecure girl, or the aloof gestures of a proud beauty who turns her head and nose aside, chin almost touching her shoulder. Neither girl communicates friendliness. Many such expressive gestures and habits disappear in private. They become apparent again only when people meet.

Trina, now eighteen, tells this story: "When I was younger, if my mother had guests, I just stayed in my room until they went home. I hated to talk to adults. I never knew what to say. My mother would always say, 'Stand up straight, Trina.'" Like many other young girls, Trina walked pulled-in to herself. She was embarrassed by her developing body. So she resorted to "hiding her breasts" to conceal her sexual drive. Other girls who want to conceal their maturing bodies wear baggy sweatshirts, loose sweaters, or smocklike tops. Some constantly pull and tug at their sweaters. They attempt to hide the shape that swells either too much or too little.

Defense and Aggression

I asked an experienced guidance counselor if any particular body language appeared universal among the young adults he counsels. "They talk without lifting their head. Some are shy, not comfortable with an adult. Others are hostile. Some slouch way down in a chair, with a defiant attitude. For others, the slouch just means they are extremely comfortable people. It all depends on the circumstances."

He also noted that girls go without shoes much of the time. Some do so to "get to their parents," and others to be comfortable. Dr. Goffman feels that groups in our culture often strive for a unique character all their own. Thus, they combine their standards in a particular way. They may have much pride in their appearance, or they may have little. Rather than abide by rules, they may take great pains to break the rules safely.

Some movements and postures say we consider ourselves superior. Pat, at eighteen, told this story: "I attended a City Council meeting recently. I was speaking as a representative for our Ecology Club, and I stretched back in my chair and crossed my hands behind my neck. I was suddenly uncomfortable, as if this posture was quite out of place. I think something in their reaction told me that. What does this gesture say?"

When questioned about the background of the situation, she recalled that she was very much in command of the conversation. She was talking confidently about the advantages of bicycle trails for which the Ecology Club had petitioned. Her gestures amplified her words. She felt superior. Do you remember seeing this gesture from others, more commonly from men? By reinforcing her superiority, she aroused defenses in her listeners. She was an astute "listener" to body language and quickly saw that the others objected to her posture. Their feedback helped her change her approach.

Dr. Albert Scheflen, writing in *Psychiatry* (a medical journal), says, "A posture such as sitting back in a chair rarely occurs in subordinate males who are engaged in selling an idea to a male of higher status."

Our outward acts of defensive behavior cause trouble in many communications. For example, Mike wanted to use the family car. His dad said he couldn't until he completed several chores he had been assigned. During the discussion, Mike felt cornered. He wanted to say, "Okay, okay, enough already. Let me go now." Instead, he looked toward the door and unconsciously turned his body slightly away from his father. This gesture irritated his father, made him think that Mike had control of the conversation and had terminated it. Mike's posture and eye movement signaled that he had already mentally closed the door on his father. When we exhibit control as Mike did, we arouse defenses in others.

His father became angry. "Don't turn away from me when I'm talking to you."

"I didn't," Mike countered. His eyes flashed anger.

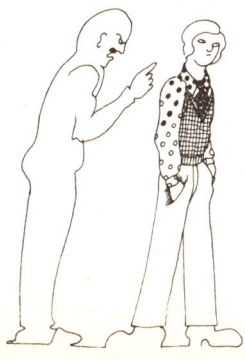

Soon the discussion became a heated argument about insolence and leaving, a total departure from the original point. Now Mike's chances of getting the car even after the chores were completed were practically nil. Yet he had not intended to anger his father. Had he been more aware of his own body language, the situation might have ended more happily. The same thing is true when a parent lets you know in no uncertain terms that he is in control of a situation, not you. This attitude arouses your anger. Real communication is blocked once more.

The way we position our bodies in relation to others sends a message. David, sixteen, sat on a rock along the beach talking to Cindy, eighteen. He was lively and interested in impressing Cindy. She rarely looked at him. Most of the time she had her shoulder distinctly turned away. She kept looking along the beach for someone more interesting. Occasionally she looked back at David. He didn't "hear" the message, that he was wasting his time. Perhaps in this case he didn't want to hear! Later that day, David's older brother pointed out how obvious the scene was. David laughed — but then agreed.

Our postures vary depending on our sex. If a man is attracted to you and wants to know you better, he will sit *facing* you. A woman would sit *next* to you. Females also appear to be more sensitive to nonverbal messages from others. A neighbor once told me this story about her sixteen-year-old daughter. "If only her father could be more sensitive to Maria's emotional state! I can tell so easily when she is upset, when she is on the brink of tears. John always says the wrong thing." We might all learn to be more aware of the silent messages sent our way when someone is depressed.

According to a University of Virginia study, a young girl's communication through body movement is influenced by her family situation. If her father is dead, or her parents are divorced, she won't develop social skills easily. She is not confident in dealing with the opposite sex. The study indicated that girls from divorced homes have unusually high heterosexual activity. When both types of girls were interviewed by a female interviewer, they all behaved similarly. When interviewed by a man, girls from a divorced home sat closer and smiled. They showed aggressive behavior. Girls whose fathers had died sat farther away, avoided eye and speech contact. They showed defensive behavior.

Our sitting and standing postures communicate far more than we realize. A posture more common to males is the straddle-a-chair position. At a rap session, when a young man sits astride a chair, with the chair back facing you, how do you feel about him? Does he seem friendly and cooperative? Or do you think he is dominant and aggressive? Researchers say he wants to dominate.

Aggressive postures sometimes really say, "I'm ready and willing." Depending on the situation, you can usually tell when someone is being pushy or cooperative. Suppose you want to choose sides for a volleyball game at the beach. The person who stands with hands on hips (a ready and willing pose) might be a good choice for your team. This person is a high achiever who expects to lead. He likes to push for a goal. This body language says, "Okay, let's go. I'm ready, what are we waiting for?"

You might also see this message when someone is seated. The person leans forward with one hand on the thigh, legs slightly apart. Suppose the Student

Council meeting drags on in a time-consuming debate. When you see Tom shift forward in the chair, his feet on tiptoes, this message says he is ready to end the discussion, to come to agreement. We should learn to recognize this sprinter's position. It says, "I'm receptive now." When we bring gestures out of our subconscious, they appear to be more meaningful. We can then receive a full message, not just a vague awareness.

All of us have been told at some time or another in a classroom, "Sit still, for heaven's sake."

No doubt we felt like responding, "Can't you see I'm bored with what you are saying?"

A huge amount of data has been collected about

fidgeters. When we can't sit still in a meeting or classroom, we are:

1. Not stimulated or interested enough to pay attention.
2. Tired or sleepy.
3. Uncomfortable in the chairs provided.
4. Preoccupied with other things.

When I taught a college class, I soon learned to tune in to body language. If I had too many fidgeters, I tried to involve the students or I called a coffee break earlier than usual.

An experienced anthropology professor and student of kinesics warned me about one student posture that I would surely have misjudged. She said, "When a student becomes deeply absorbed in the subject, he slips way down on his shoulder blades, sprawls his feet apart. He doesn't look at me at all. Rather he stares at the floor or his table. He seems almost to be in a trance. But I know he is more likely to be with me than someone sitting bolt upright." Had Dr. Jacobs not warned me, I would have supposed this student had tuned out. When the student sits up, rearranges his clothes, and smooths his hair, he has stopped concentrating.

Leadership

Kinesic investigators have some interesting theories about leadership qualities and the use of body language. In a study on leadership, three boys in a high-school group were singled out as "heavy vocalizers." We might consider all of these boys loudmouths. In fifteen film-recorded sessions, these three were responsible for from seventy-two to ninety-three percent of all the words spoken. But only one of them actually had real leadership qualities. He initiated more conversation and thought trends than any other boy.

However, another boy in the group — let's call him Steve — who was thought to have high leadership qualities, had one of the lowest word counts. He began conversations at an average rate, but he spoke only sixteen percent of the words. His leadership, researchers say, was a kinesic one. He was kinesically more mature. Although he talked relatively little, he held the reputation of being a good conversationalist. Steve was a good listener. He did not send negative signals, such as leg shuffling and foot jiggling. He could steer the conversation along with proper head and face movements. When he spoke, he didn't put his hands around his mouth, scratch his head, or cross his arms. A mature person moves with a purpose. Too many body gestures without real meaning say, "I'm restless, not interested." They also say that the person is immature.

Inclusion or Exclusion

Even without words, one can see a wide variety of human relationships in progress. Experts in kinesics say there are three basic dimensions to postures in interaction. These dimensions, which all occur at the same time in any unit of posture, are:

1. Inclusiveness or noninclusiveness of posture. This quality defines the area for the activities and marks access to the group.

2. Face-to-face or parallel body positions. The choice between the two tells about the types of social activities going on. Face-to-face postures are sometimes called vis-a-vis postures by kinesicists.

3. Congruence or noncongruence (harmony or nonharmony) of stance and limbs shows association or disassociation of group members.

The first dimension of inclusiveness or noninclusiveness defines the group by body placement. If members are standing, as at a party, they tend to form a circle. This position excludes all others. Or, if they are in a line, the members at each end turn inward and place an arm or leg across the open space, "bookending" the group. This position cuts off intruders. In American groups, males usually sit on the ends of a seated group, as on a couch. Often the man of highest status will assume the end position. He acts as protector of the group. Body placement may also effectively keep little subgroups from forming. We sometimes place our bodies as barriers to keep two people from flirting — or from arguing. If two people are known to dislike each other, others may try to separate them. They may put a leg up on a piece of furniture, or two people may cross their legs to "box in" the person to be controlled.

If people assume face-to-face postures, a certain type of social interaction usually takes place, such as conversation, courtship, teaching, or arguing. Parallel postures find people sitting or standing side by side, reading, watching television, or doing something that could just as easily be carried out alone.

The third category, congruence-noncongruence, is concerned with the ways that people imitate each other or disagree with each other. Two or more people in a small group may sit with their legs crossed at the knee, their arms stretched out comfortably, and their heads cocked to one side. They may be, in body postures, carbon copies of each other or mirror images. Congruent, or in-harmony, postures may happen in either face-to-face or parallel situations.

Think of yourself at a rap session sometime. Look around the room to see if you can spot two sides in a discussion. Persons with a common viewpoint will often adopt the same posture. Unconsciously you tend to mirror the image with which you identify. If the discussion becomes a heated argument, sides may be easy to spot. In a group of three or more people, two basic arrangements of postures are commonly seen. When one member of a congruent set shifts posture, the others who agree with him will quickly follow suit. The harmony may be maintained through repeated changes of body position. A sudden change in posture often signals a changing mind. The person whose posture differs from the others, or is non-congruent, probably disagrees with them.

One other significance of out-of-harmony posture is the indication of status. A school counselor I know deliberately adopts a different posture, to show his status is higher than that of the students. He stretches back in his chair and links his hands behind his head. He comments, "I am the counselor and friend, but not the same as a buddy."

In family counseling, therapists sometimes see two sets of congruent posture, which show two subgroups within the family. One child may follow the postures of the mother, while the others are in harmony with the father.

Though not infallible, scientists tell us these signs are worth a closer look. When you speak at a club meeting, watch the postures of those around you. A person may quickly uncross her legs as a response when you say something that startles or stimulates. Remember, however, that her response may be to an extraneous stimulation, such as discomfort in her legs. Scientists are quick to warn that when a shift in postures takes place, something is happening, but we cannot specifically say that one posture means only one thing.

Dr. Scheflen points out that a shift in posture is "like a referee's whistle at the end of a play in football. It means that some unit is ended, but does not identify the unit. Or it can be likened to the ringing of a church bell in a small Italian town." The townspeople are told that something is happening, but they need more information to know what.

The study of human communications is still in its infancy. Surprising things have already been learned about this complicated nonverbal code. Perhaps someday we will learn to control our kinesic behavior in the same way that we control our verbal behavior.

CHAPTER SIX

The Courting Game

So court a mistress, she denies you;
Let her alone, she will court you.
BEN JONSON

Body movements communicate in many different ways, and scientists are now beginning to find just how the nonverbal code works. What surprises many of us is that we are so physically sensitive to each other. Sometimes we pick up a feeling of closeness to someone from their body language. At other times we feel definitely rebuffed.

We all know that people in love look at each other longer and sit or stand much closer together. When two people respond to each other, some of the ways are familiar and others are quite subtle.

Sixteen-year-old Beverly tells this story: "At the park the other day I was introduced to a really handsome older boy. We had a long conversation about the new kinds of tennis rackets. That's the only thing we talked about. Yet I suddenly felt sure that he was really interested in me — not the tennis rackets at all." His body language, from eye contact to alert muscle tone, told Beverly that he was "courting."

Some of the subtle ways we court each other have been analyzed in great detail by Dr. Albert Scheflen. He says that there are visible changes in the way a person holds his body. Our eyes seem to be brighter.

Muscles snap to attention, and any sagging or slumping disappears or decreases. A woman in love seems to be more beautiful, he feels; even her skin takes on new tone. A woman's legs may become sleek, like those we see in cheesecake photos or on a professional model. Jowls, as well as bagginess around the eyes, disappear. Potbellies seem to be tucked in when people are ready for courtship.

Dr. Birdwhistell also notes that attractiveness is a transitory thing, like sunshine on a cloudy day. Love can make a woman look quite beautiful for a brief time. Or we can become very ugly in times of anger and hate.

Another anthropologist says she "can tell from the way a couple stand and walk together how intimate they are." Body movement and muscle tone, especially in their thighs, she feels, are telltale signs.

In *Psychiatry* (a medical journal), Dr. Scheflen says of American courting behavior elements, "They appeared not only among lovers, but in psychotherapy sessions, business meetings, parties, conferences, and so on." Many of our courting movements are accompanied by other gestures that serve as "qualifiers," when they are used in situations that are not meant to be either seductive or sexual.

Typical Courting Gestures

First, let's look at some typical courting gestures intended to be seductive. A courting female may stroke her hair or play with it. She may twist one strand around her finger. Men usually comb or stroke their hair. They also button or readjust a coat or sweater, and they pull up their socks. These movements are termed *preening* gestures. They are seen in early stages of courtship readiness.

Attractive, shapely Mia corners Mike at a party. She strokes her hair. Then she brings her hand to touch a golden earring, ending with her palm facing him. He returns the greeting, adjusting his tie, as he answers this subtle female courting with a male courting movement. "Whether she knows it or not, when a female shows you her palm, she's courting you," Dr. Scheflen explains. She seeks an encounter, even if only in a business way. Whether Mia continues to court in a sexual way will depend on whether she adds any qualifiers to her body messages.

Dr. Scheflen points out that American women normally show their palm very little, "but in courting, they palm all over the place, even to covering a cough with palm out."

Women seldom use the preening gestures in company of their own sex, but in mixed company they are not hard to spot. Women also protrude their breasts, tip their heads to a flirty angle, roll their hips, and walk with a pelvic sway. "Crossing the legs, to slightly expose the thigh, placing a hand on the hip, and showing the wrist or palm are also invitational. Slow stroking motions of the fingers on the thigh or wrist also are common," according to Dr. Scheflen.

After the initial stages of courtship, Dr. Scheflen has observed that a second step takes place. When a male and female have established that they are attracted to each other, they proceed to a "positioning for courtship." The partners turn their bodies and heads to face one another, in a tête-à-tête position. They lean toward each other. They block off others by placing their chairs or limbs in a certain way. Conversation takes on an intimate tone now. If a third person is present, the courting twosome may open the position of the upper half of their bodies to include him. They then form a closed circle with their legs by crossing their feet toward each other. This formation, in effect, blocks out the intruder from the private happening. The open position of their upper bodies seems to be a surrender to social responsibility.

The Qualifiers

Now let's consider the courting behavior that rules out any sexual implications. Dr. Scheflen calls it "quasi-courtship," or a seeming-to-court behavior. The same signals may be sent between two people, but a qualifier, or disclaimer, is added. Two people at a party may be displaying one courtship gesture after another. Then suddenly the female will mention her steady boyfriend, as if to remind the male that they are only friends. Or she may look around the room with her eyes in search of a third party. Should she fail to add the qualifiers, then she may not rightly later protest to his continued sexual advances. Misunderstandings happen sometimes when a girl vacillates about her own intentions. She may unconsciously forget to qualify her actions. This omission is possibly a clue to her real intentions. Experts say, if she intended her behavior to be merely a quasi-courtship, the evidence would have been there from the beginning.

There are other methods to make clear that a sexual encounter is not expected. Omitting some key part of the message is a common qualifier, says Dr. Scheflen. For example, in courtship a man may lean forward, touch his partner, soften his facial expression, and softly speak of his love. In quasi-courting, he may say the same words while he leans slightly away from her and smiles only with his lips without crinkling his eyes. He may use a matter-of-fact tone of voice. If your boyfriend leans away from you, you will probably pick up the signal that something is wrong in your relationship, even though you may not actually notice *what* he did to give you this feeling.

Quasi-courting happens in nearly any situation, from the classroom to the business meeting, between parents and children, between teachers and students, between doctors and patients. It occurs between members of the same sex as well as between opposite sexes. This ritual has been described by one expert as a "deliberate game for enhancing attractiveness and social interest." Such courting takes place across marital lines quite commonly. As long as certain rules are observed, it does not produce anxiety or tension. But the alarm bell rings if one party excludes others, seeks isolation, begins to form complete postures with a partner, and tries to make contact by touching. Then the quasi-courtship may be changing into an actual courtship.

In a school situation between a female student and a male teacher perhaps a routine meeting is taking place. Yet a certain sexuality runs through the conversation. Both are well aware of the sexual difference between them. However, qualifiers probably will be present. One person could turn his body somewhat away from the other. Or he could omit certain eye contact, which would be present in actual courtship. Of course, some people are not aware of the signals that qualify a relationship. They think any advance is sexual. They begin to respond accordingly with their own courting devices turned up to high volume. Or they may suddenly freeze up and start to send "decourting" gestures fast and furiously. When decourting, muscle tone changes and coquettish behavior may come to an abrupt end. Indeed, barriers may be set up in a situation that goes too far too fast. A girl may quickly put her arm across her lap, or she may cross her arms and tightly twist her legs.

Dr. Scheflen explains that sometimes in psychotherapy a doctor will openly use quasi-courting to involve his patients, especially when they are schizophrenics. He may use this flirting bahavior, such as tie adjustment or other male preening, to get a young girl to talk openly or to interest her in the therapy session. He describes a session in which a mother, daughter, grandmother, and father visited the therapist. During the many times the therapist began to talk to either the daughter or the grandmother, the mother moved into courtship readiness with coquettish body language. She crossed her legs, extended them, placed her hand on her hip, and leaned forward.

The therapist responded to her preening. He turned to the mother and began a conversation. Both the daughter and the granddaughter immediately placed a leg across the space between the mother and the doctor, "boxing in" the mother. The mother then decourted, sitting back, losing muscle tone, and dropping her coquettish behavior. The daughter and grandmother boxed in the flirting mother after a foot-waving signal from the father.

This entire charade was carried out in filmed therapy, although none of the parties involved was aware of her signaling. The same behavior was repeated many times during the session.

Courting Gestures in Other Situations

Some women constantly assume or imitate the appearance of courtship readiness, according to Dr. Scheflen. They may wear slightly bizarre clothes or wear shoes that throw the feet and legs into taut muscle tone. By their cosmetics, too, such women give the impression of sexiness. Experienced men, this researcher feels, "recognize that a 'sexy' woman is not necessarily sexual. She is, perhaps, even likely to be frigid." Her appearance is not in any way a response to a man. Many men, therefore, flock to this female because they feel safe. They know that this siren in the low-cut dress who seems to attract men does not wish to get involved. Nonsexual courting also happens at a meeting or a party when one person either withdraws or for some reason is excluded. The withdrawn member may be called back by touch or in other quasi-courting ways. In therapy films, researchers noted that this courting was evident regularly. For example, in one session the young daughter at first flashed courting signals at the therapist. When he avoided talking to her or responding to her courting, she gradually lost interest. She sat back and did not seem to care about the session. Soon after, although the therapist was not able to talk to her, he locked glances with her. He held her eyes while both dragged on their cigarettes in perfect synchrony. Possibly she became self-conscious about this near intimacy, for she suddenly placed an arm across her lap and looked away. But she did not, from then on, withdraw from the group.

We have all seen the effect of an attractive person pumping life into what had been a dull meeting or a dull evening until his arrival. This ability is the effect of quasi-courting in a social setting, kinesic experts tell us. The state is thought to be necessary to allow a group to "become animated and cohesive enough to work together to complete a dull or tedious task." The attractive person acts as a catalyst to bring out the best in others through his own sociability, readiness to relate, and attentiveness. Psychologists think that the underlying state of sociability and relating to others is basically sexual.

Sexual and nonsexual advances, scientists say, can be readily confused. Some of us seem only to provoke and imagine sexual advances from others. You might call this person a "tease." She is constantly seductive, even when she is not supposed to be. She has no intention of following through on her actions.

Some people do not seem able to deal with the leavening aspects of quasi-courting, says Dr. Scheflen. "They ignore the qualifiers." They respond by freezing, withdrawing, or criticizing. These people feel alienated and seem to disturb any group they join. Perhaps the person who often gets into trouble socially is not reading the body language correctly either consciously or unconsciously.

A fair amount of learning, much of it on the unconscious level, is needed to see the crucial differences and to make proper interpretations between sexual and nonsexual courting behavior.

CHAPTER SEVEN

To Touch or Not to Touch

No man is an island.
JOHN DONNE

Do you recall being comforted by your mother when you were a small child? She probably said something reassuring like, "There, there, everything will be all right now," as she patted you on the back. She touched you in some way.

The sense of touch is our most primitive sense. Yet scientists made few attempts to study it until the twentieth century. We have just begun to realize the importance of touching, of tactile communication.

If someone touches you on the arm, you are aware of some message. When skin contacts skin, either directly or through layers of cloth, we have a sensory awareness. The sender and the receiver may experience different meanings from that touch. Before we can understand the meaning of someone's touch, we must consider the whole situation. Did someone gently hold your hand? Did they grab you by the arm? Or did they merely brush against your arm in passing? The part of the body touched is significant, too. A hand that rests on your knee says something quite different from a hand that lightly rests on your arm.

Imagine you are at an awards banquet. Someone you did not like was coming toward you. He greeted everyone around you with a brief handclasp. But he did not take your hand. The absence of a handshake where one is expected can be shattering. This lack of touch says more than a swift kick in the shins. George Bernard Shaw once said, "Silence is the most perfect expression of scorn." Your enemy chose to be silent in his body language. Yet the message shouted at you.

Function of Skin

The word *touch* is the longest single entry in the Oxford English Dictionary. One definition reads: "The most general of the bodily senses, diffused through all parts of the skin, but (in man) specially developed in the tips of the fingers and the lips."

Tactile experiences begin early on the evolutionary scale. Tiny blind creatures feel their way through life. One of the first experiences of the unborn human embryo, before eyes develop, is the sensation of being touched. While the embryo is less than eight weeks old, barely one inch long, it responds to stroking. When the tiny form of life is tickled lightly on the upper lip or near the nose, it bends its neck as if to move away from the tickling.

Our understanding of touch has evolved over many years. In the nineteenth century in the United States, babies in institutions lacked tender loving care. The mortality rate was shocking—nearly 100 percent in infants under one year old. Babies died from a disease called *maramus*, a Greek word that means *wasting away*.

Some doctors recognized the emotional emptiness in hospitals and institutions. Few did anything about it. Dr. Fritz Talbot of Boston brought the idea of tenderness back with him from a visit to Germany. He had toured the wards there in a children's clinic. A fat, waddling old woman carried a scrawny infant about on her hip. He asked about the woman. "That's old Anna," he was told. "When all else fails, and we have done everything medically possible, then we turn the baby over to old Anna. She's always successful."

Americans at that time in our history thought that handling a baby other than for clocklike bottle feedings would result in a spoiled child. To put a baby in a cradle and touch him often was an unscientific thing to do. Not until the 1920's did the idea of mothering and cuddling infants in hospital wards take hold. In one year, mortality rates dropped by more than twenty-five percent.

From birth, babies need to be held and touched. Children who are deprived of touch in infancy may grow up emotionally and mentally stunted. Anthropologist Dr. Ashley Montagu, in his book *Touching*, writes that, "We are conscious of satisfying a baby's needs for hunger, thirst, sleep, and avoidance of dangerous things. But we need to be more aware of the tactile needs, for healthy growth and development."

We are in constant contact with the outside world through our skin. Sun, air pressure, wind, and cold all bombard us through our skin, an extraordinary sensory detector. Dr. Montagu says that "Poems have been written in celebration of every part of the body, but the skin unaccountably appears to have been slighted, as if it did not exist."

Yet many common expressions show that we are well aware of the tactile functions of our skin. We say someone is a "soft touch," or we mention "rubbing people the wrong way." We say, "keep in touch," or that "I'm deeply touched." Sometimes people say, "He gets under my skin." Some of us are "thin-skinned" or "touchy" (too sensitive), while some of us are "thick-skinned" (tough minded, not offended easily).

Most of what we now know about the function of our skin has been learned since 1940. Primarily scientists are concerned with what kind of skin experiences and stimulations are needed for healthy development. Is behavior affected by lack of touching experiences? Does touching cause our physical growth to change in response?

Researchers have done many investigations in the animal world to learn more about both animal and human skin responses. In an experiment with rats, thyroid and parathyroid glands were removed. Some of the rats died, while others did not. Inquiry showed that rats were taken from two different colonies. One group came from the Experimental Colony where rats were petted, handled, and "gentled." Another group, called Standard Stock rats, were touched only for routine feeding and cage cleaning. Both groups were caged in the same manner and fed the same diet.

The Standard Stock rats' typical behavior was nervous, frightened, tense. They were timid and withdrawn. When an attendant picked up these rats, they would bite or go into a rage. The gentled rats had strikingly different behavior. They were not afraid when picked up. They were calm and secure. These rats had been stroked, talked to, handled.

Sixty-six percent more of the Standard Stock rats died after the surgery than did the gentled rats. Experiments proved that the more handling and touching rats receive, the better they do in a laboratory situation. In a series of research projects with rats in Denver, Dr. Alfred F. Washburn commented, "It sounds silly, but petted rats learned faster and grew faster."

Animals love to be stroked, especially dogs and cats. Dolphins also show this response. Cows that are hand milked rather than machine milked give more and richer milk.

Do human beings respond to touch in the same ways that animals do? Babies explore their whole world with the sense of touch. When a baby begins to move around, his sense of touch serves as his earliest guide. He touches a hard surface or finds a warm or cold surface. He touches people on all parts of their bodies. A baby suffers stress in the birth process. Immediately after being squeezed from a warm and comforting place, the baby is taken from its mother and placed in an incubator or in the wide open spaces of a crib. Many researchers feel that the baby should be placed in the warmth of his mother's arms instead. Anthropologist Margaret Mead calls this major shock of birth "skin shock." Scientists say that, when we pull blankets close around us, we reflect our desire to re-create the conditions of the womb, where warm fluid enclosed us.

Babies sense when their mother is nervous or tense by skin contact. If a baby is to thrive, the messages it receives should be pleasant ones. As a baby grows older, the mother's words and voice take the place of close physical contacts.

Skin Hunger

American mothers make the most tactile communication with their children when the child is fourteen months to two years old. This touching contact steadily declines with age. Girl babies receive more open affection than boy babies do. Girl babies also are weaned later than boys. Researchers say this fact could account for the American female being so much less tense about touching than American males. Mothers have a more indulgent attitude toward girls. Fathers normally show little tactile affection to their sons.

Some families have a great deal of tactile contact, while others have very little. I once heard a family described as a "very kissy family." Sometimes whole cultures have a don't-touch-me attitude, while others have an enormous amount of touching. For example, Balinese babies are carried around with their mother in a slinglike device. They have constant skin contact for the first two years. These babies feel the rocking, rhythmic movements of the mother. While the mother pounds her rice, the baby adjusts to her every stroke.

In contrast, infants in our culture spend the most part of their waking hours and all of their sleeping time alone or away from others. According to Dr. Montagu, because of their early tactile experiences, Balinese children feel they can always return to "the known arms of parents and siblings, where fright and comfort, interest and sleep, have already been experienced."

Young children in the Western world frequently come into their parents' bed at night for comfort. Many toddlers have trouble falling asleep. They ask to be tucked in, to have a drink, to hear a story, or to have someone lie beside them while they fall asleep. They show a great need for close human contact, a desire for touching. Many researchers feel this comfort should be given to the child. Gradually he will outgrow the need for this reassurance.

Among children, the fear of falling may also be related to touch. Youngsters who were not securely held as infants show anxiety over high places, like swings or slides. A healthy child likes to be tossed in the air and caught by a parent. But a child who suffers from little tactile stimulation may carry with him a fear of falling for much of his life. Some psychiatrists think this person worries about losing control of his body, which includes the fear of falling in love.

When a child is deprived of touch as an infant he develops habits to compensate for this lack. He may suck his thumb, pull his hair, pick his nose, or chew his fingers. Among nonliterate peoples, who give much tactile stimulation to babies, these habits rarely occur.

As we approach our teens, we are less likely to seek or receive touching contact from our parents. Then in our teens and early twenties, we feel a new surge of touching sensitivity. Rock-and-roll music, according to Dr. Montagu, is possibly a "compensatory effect of the lack of parents' attention to cutaneous (skin) needs." Dances like the twist and other rock variations could represent reaction to lack of early tactile stimulation. Lyrics are often addressed to the older generation. They may express sentiments such as, "You don't understand." Our need for touch at this time of life is part of our search for acceptance and reassurance.

The need for body contact accelerates during stress. In a psychiatric study, doctors found that at least one half of the women involved had used sex to get a man to hold them. One woman described her need to be held as a "kind of ache... not an emotional longing for some person who isn't there; it's a physical feeling." Sexual experiences of unhappy people seem to be an attempt to make some sort of touching contact. The need to be held and cuddled is acceptable only as part of adult sexuality. So some women convert this longing to be held into acceptable behavior by establishing sexual relationships.

Girls sometimes complain that boys are rough and clumsy at touching. Experts say this inability could "reflect the lack of tactile experiences many males have suffered in childhood." Twelve-year-old Donna described typical boy behavior. "If a boy likes you," she said, "he'll probably kick you, on the playground." Other girls say boys punch them on the arm or pull their hair to show they like the girl. Boys get a girl's attention this way, and they make a clumsy attempt to touch.

At a juvenile home, Sally told this story: "I know I shouldn't do it, but I feel this urge to have a boy hold me tight, just hug me. Sometimes I say, 'Just hold me, just hold me.' They always think I want something more. I don't."

Sally's story is not an unusual one. Yet other young adults, both boys and girls, claim they can't develop contact relationships with anyone. "As soon as he tries to touch me in any way, I freeze," Jill explained.

"The idea of touching, of being really close to a girl," says Carl, "scares me to death."

Both cases, psychologists say, show the result of lack of tactile stimulation as infants. Now both Jill and Carl are awkward in body relations with others. To embrace, kiss, or make any touching contact arouses guilt, disgust, or shame. Advice columnists frequently get letters from adults whose mates suffer from such tactile failure.

Dr. Alexander Lowen feels that our expressions of sex are all, more or less, influenced by our early tactile experience. He points out, in his book *Physical Dynamics of Character Study*, "The quality of physical intimacy between mother and child reflects the mother's feelings about the intimacy of sex." If the mother feels that sex is dirty, her body contact shows this feeling. If she is ashamed of her body, she won't want to nurse her baby or will do so begrudgingly. When she bathes or diapers the baby, she finds touching the genitals repugnant. The child then also develops a feeling of shame about his own body.

Our needs to be touched vary. They seem to differ depending upon how we were satisfied in childhood. *Tactile failure*, as scientists call lack of touching, often results in emotional shallowness. People suffering from this very real need may become adults who cannot form close relationships with anyone. They cannot be in touch.

Handshakes and Tickling

A handshake is a way of touching that we see repeated hundreds of times a day in our culture. This greeting is a modification of the primitive gesture in which both hands were raised to show that the person held no weapons. Our modern handshake is a clinging to each other, a gesture of welcome. It says, "We belong together. We are as one, even though we may be of a different rank." Our palms interlock to show openness.

We expect a certain amount of pressure or firmness in a handshake. If pressure is not returned, we feel let down. We say a person has a "dead fish" handshake. Young boys are taught by their fathers to "give a good squeeze" when they shake hands. Women, especially in the business world, develop a firm handshake out of self-defense. They increasingly shake hands when introduced to men, even on social occasions. An attractive female executive said, "It gives a feeling of warmth to shake hands in greeting."

A politician shakes hands in other ways, often using two hands. He grasps your hand with his right hand, then cups his left around it on top. Or he may place his left hand on your forearm as he shakes with his right hand. This way of touching sometimes makes us think that he tries too hard to make us like him.

Young adults have developed a variety of semi-secret handshakes. They are reserved for either their peers or for an older person whom they might consider "with it." One popular handshake of this type starts out like a conventional handshake; then one hand wraps around the thumb of the other person's hand. This gesture may satisfy the need to enter into "collusive intimacy," in social scientist Dr. Erving Goffman's terms. It determines the outsiders of our group.

Tickling is a special type of touching contact. Some researchers consider it primarily a sexual action. When someone tries to tickle you, he shows aggression, a desire to touch. In our culture, playful boys in early adolescence tickle each other to test their masculinity. If a boy giggles, he is not quite a man. He is a sissy. If he is manly, he controls himself. When tickling, someone may touch your ribs or back of the neck. These parts of the body are not normally touched by others.

Some Special Touches

Many gestures in which we touch ourselves are in some way self-comforting. Our nose seems to be a favored place of contact when we need to reassure ourselves. We wring our hands, rub our thumb and index finger together. We rub our thumb or fingers against our other palm.

Some tactile gestures send a message of affection. When we pat someone's cheek or hair, we are saying, "I like you."

Suppose you are upset about a physical problem and you are in your doctor's office. He tries to explain something. Then he pats your hand. This touch has a soothing effect when we are in distress. Often in conversation you see someone reach out and touch another. The gesture says, "Now, now, everything will be okay." Experts tell us that most touchers show their emotions readily. They are especially quick to demonstrate them to people whom they like.

Sometimes a reach-and-touch-the-forearm gesture in conversation is an interruption signal or is used to emphasize a point.

Touch communicates some interesting things among couples in a group or at a party. Joan and Bob, a steady twosome for nearly a year, signal that their relationship is sometimes strained. Bob accuses Joan of being a flirt at parties. When Joan seems to enjoy a lively chitchat with another boy, Bob quickly moves closer to her, puts his arm around her waist, or drapes his arm around her shoulder. Bob squeezes Joan's upper arm, as if to remind her that she belongs to him. His nonverbal message lets everyone know he is possessive. He is concerned that Joan may be paying too much attention to others.

Bob moves around the party holding Joan's hand, another this-is-mine signal. When Bob goes to get a Coke for Joan, she talks with another boy. Her hand and arm are stretched along the back of a sofa. Bob comes back, sets the Cokes on a table, and places his hand over Joan's. She abruptly withdraws her hand. This body language shows that she is annoyed at his possessiveness. Her hand extends to another boy to show that she is interested in him. Clearly the steady twosome is cooling in her mind. She also slightly shrugs her shoulders when Bob puts his arm around her, as if to be rid of an annoyance. Unaware, Bob merely asks, "Are you cold, honey?"

Kinesic researchers say that couples who have had a quarrel are often quite formal to each other at a party. They touch very little, or if one reaches out, the other responds by withdrawing the hand or arm touched. Dr. Edward Hall wrote in *Hidden Dimension* that "the hardened, armorlike resistance to the unwanted touch...is a message of one body to another that has universal meaning."

Some females need constant reassurance of a relationship through touch. Have you ever seen a girl "hanging all over her boyfriend"? Nancy, who has just begun dating, feels compelled to hang on Bill's arm or to have her arm around him all the time. Bill is considered a prize catch, and Nancy is proud to be seen with him. She signals ownership, as well as the need for security. This behavior can be stifling.

Dr. Haim Ginott in *Between Parent and Teenager* told this story: Jean walked along the beach with her mother. She asked, "Mom, how do you hold a husband after you've finally gotten him?"

Her mother gave her a silent lesson in love. She scooped up two handfuls of sand. One she squeezed hard. The more she squeezed, the more sand escaped. The other she held lightly, and the sand remained.

Jean said, "I see."

Our society has placed taboos on touch. We often equate physical contact with sex, even though in some situations a sexual message is clearly not intended. Perhaps this attitude explains why we use touching so sparingly to show warmth and affection.

One extensive study showed that ninety percent of students from seven to ten years old welcome hugging and patting from their teacher. Older students seem to know that our culture frowns on this conduct.

If we touch someone, we immediately apologize. Anticontact behavior, according to some experts, helps keep the number of our acquaintances to the proper level for our species. Dr. Desmond Morris in *The Naked Ape* says, "We do this with remarkable consistency and uniformity. We keep our acquaintances to something like a small tribal group, in line with basic biological rules of our ancient ancestors," he continues. We appear to have changed very little since our early primitive days.

In Catholic churches something new has been added to the service. The priest says, "Shall we offer each other a sign of peace?" Then each person gives his hand to others around him, as he says something similar to "Peace be with you." Not surprisingly, most people are slightly embarrassed to reach out and touch a stranger, even a fellow parishioner. They may also act quite formally to members of their own family when touching is expected.

A young priest made this comment, "How can we expect to touch the lives of a total stranger, when we are even ill at ease in touching the person next to us in church?"

Dr. Montagu says, "To get in touch, in a very real sense, we must be able to embrace and enjoy the embraces of others." This capability is one measure of our development as a healthy human being. If we are deprived of touch, we are not only physically awkward; we also become "tactless" in later life.

Some behavioral scientists feel we are in a time of "skin hunger." Encounter groups and drug culture seem to be attempts to get back in touch with another human body. In encounters, participants hold and touch one another. They are urged to do so, to make contact physically. Ritual gatherings like music festivals crowd people together in an animal warmth of close bodies. But not only the young need the warmth of contact. The aged especially suffer from skin hunger; lack of touch isolates them from life around them.

As we have briefly seen, not only our words, but also our acts of touch communicate involvement and response—powerful needs for both young and old.

CHAPTER EIGHT

Space Needs

*I want, by understanding myself,
to understand others.*
KATHERINE MANSFIELD

Each of us walks around in an individual space zone, a territory that belongs uniquely to us. This space zone has been called our private space bubble. Others may not intrude unless invited. What happens when our space bubble is threatened? Do we defend our territory? Do we become aggressive, or do we crouch and withdraw? What happens to communications when two people misunderstand space needs?

Each of these questions is a part of nonverbal communication. Scientists are beginning to learn how our use of space communicates to others. Our concept of space around us sends a silent message on matters from status to expression of personality. If we understand our own space bubble, we will also see how we intrude on others' private territory. We carry our space bubble with us. It changes in size and shape depending on the circumstances.

For example, when people line up to see a wholesome family movie like *Sound of Music*, they will stand about one foot apart. For a sex comedy such as *Tom Jones*, people will stand very close. About 350 people cram their bodies together in the same amount of space that would handle only 125 people for a family movie. Our space bubble appears to shrink if we expect to see something earthy. It shrinks also when lights are dim. We do not mind moving close together at an intimate restaurant when lights are low. Or we turn the lights down to create a cozy party atmosphere, to help people get closer to each other.

A Sense of Territory

Dr. Edward Hall has coined the word *proxemics* to describe his theories about our use of space. To help understand our space needs, we might take a closer look at animal territories. Animals, birds, fish, and primates all have an instinctive sense of territory, a given area with boundaries in which they move. Territories may vary with the season and with the food supply for some animals. For others, territory is a permanent fact.

According to anthropologist Hall, human beings have developed their territoriality to an unbelievable extent. He defines territoriality as "laying claim to and defending a territory." Like sex, our space is there, but we seldom talk about it. At some time or other we have all seen the man of the house apologize about "his" chair. Have you ever seen someone head for the largest, most comfortable-looking chair in the room? Did he stop and say, "Oh, I almost took your chair, didn't I?" Perhaps the chair's owner was annoyed. Yet he acted polite and held back his true feelings. He could hardly say, "Darn right, that's my chair. I don't like anybody else using it!"

Whatever the need for territory among people, it appears to be even more vital among animals. Wild animals, birds, barnyard animals, and dogs staunchly defend their territory. The sense of territory, according to studies of the animal world, helps to maintain nature's balance. It offers protection from predators. It also offers a safe home base for breeding. One important function of territoriality is proper spacing. It ensures that the correct number of that species live in a given area. Each needs a certain amount of space to thrive. Beyond what the environment can support, a crisis develops. Crowding interferes with breeding and reproduction.

Weird animal behavior caused by crowding has been noted for many years. At peak of population growth, lemmings (an arctic rodent) have marched into the sea to drown. From deer to rabbits, these large-scale die-offs have happened, although food was abundant. In 1950, scientist John Christian found evidence that when animal populations in an area increase to a certain point, stress builds up. Stress from overcrowding creates an endocrine (glandular) reaction, which then causes population collapse.

Experiments in crowding have been carried out with Norway rats. When they were overcrowded, disorder and chaos were the rule. Females could not rear their young. Pregnancies decreased; fighting and tail biting were common. Social and sexual behavior deteriorated. The weak died off.

Animals define their territories in many ways. Some leave glandular scents on their zone, while others urinate to mark off their territory. We also mark off our territories. Desmond Morris, zoologist and researcher, says that we decorate our homes and fill them with personal things for this reason. Dr. Morris explains, "When you hang a painting on a wall, put a name on the door, you are in dog or wolf terms, simply cocking your leg on them and leaving your personal mark." Cars have mascots or symbols to personalize them. We fix up our room or our school locker with pictures, signs, and posters to define it as ours alone. Dr. Morris also feels that the person who obsessively collects objects often has an abnormal need to define his home territory.

As we can see, man's space zone is a set of expanding and shrinking fields that can provide information about him. This information can help us better understand behavior and personalities. Each of us has his own territorial needs. Dr. Hall says that there are four specific zones in which we function. Each zone has a close and a far phase. These zones are: 1, Intimate Distance; 2, Personal Distance; 3, Social Distance; 4, Public Distance.

Intimate Distance can be close, actually touching, or as far as six to eighteen inches away. In close intimate distance, we are sometimes overwhelmed by another's presence. We hug, kiss, or wrestle at close intimate range. A child may snuggle close to someone at this distance. Muscles of the body make contact. We comfort and protect someone.

At far intimate distance, hands can reach out and grasp each other. Americans are uncomfortable if others are in this zone when they haven't been invited. Crowded subways, elevators, and buses can put strangers into this intimate spatial zone. We have defenses to control our intimacy, though. We tense our muscles, making them rigid, and look away.

If we bump against someone in a crowded space, we quickly draw away, as if to say, "You understand I did not want to rub against you, but this situation forces it." If a man leans against a woman and appears to enjoy relaxing against her, she would probably give him an indignant shove.

Personal Distance is that small protective sphere we have around us, our private space bubble. In the close phase (from one and one-half to two and one-half feet), we get noticeable feedback from someone's eyes. How close we stand to each other signals what our relationship is and how we feel about each other. A wife can stay inside her husband's close personal zone. A girl may stay inside her boyfriend's zone. But if some other female enters this space, that's another story.

In the far phase of personal distance (from two and one-half to four feet), we are "keeping a person at arm's length." This is what we use when we talk with someone on the street. At a party, though, we might move closer.

At Social Distance nobody touches or expects to be touched unless he makes a special effort. In the close phase (four to seven feet), we do our impersonal business. When we work together or when we have casual social gatherings, we stand at this distance. When a teacher stands and looks down at you from social distance, she intends to dominate you.

In the far phase (from seven to twelve feet), we do more formal business. In such a conversation we maintain eye contact. To look away from time to time shuts off the conversation or appears rude. People in the same room doing separate things sit at about this distance. Each can read, then look up from time to time to talk.

When in Public Distance we are not personally involved with others. In the close phase (twelve to twenty-five feet), we may be in a room where a teacher talks to an entire class or at a conference where a formal speech is given. The voice is loud, but not full volume.

In the far phase (twenty-five feet or more), we must exaggerate or amplify our voice and gestures to send any real message. Actors on a stage, public figures, or anyone using a public occasion to communicate use this distance.

These four zones have been set by observations of animal and human behavior. Anthropologist Hall says that the specific distance we choose at any time depends on what is happening, how we feel about those around us, how they feel about us, and on what we are doing. Our body zones, as a result, are actual extensions of our personality. Or, as one communications specialist says, "Our sense of self is not bounded by our skin."

Our Space Bubble

Our space bubble is actually that amount of air space we need between us and another person. Anyone can demonstrate this need easily by moving in on someone. You can simply keep walking until someone complains. Or, if you have the nerve, try this test. When you enter a waiting room in which many chairs are vacant and only a few people are present, look around briefly. Then take the chair just beside someone, in spite of the vacant seats. Unnerved, he will fidget. You have breached his space bubble. His eyes will probably blink rapidly in minute tremors.

He may cross and uncross his arms and legs. Soon he will find an excuse to move. He may reach for a magazine or go talk to the receptionist. He may decide to go outside for some fresh air. Keep cool. Just tell him you were conducting a scientific experiment.

Usually when someone intrudes upon us, we are not quite aware that we have any right to be indignant or angry and we react in different ways. Some of us shrug and forget it. Others feel embarrassed, uncomfortable, as though we have done something wrong. Still others glare aggressively. A feisty sort might say, "What do you think you're doing, buddy?" A fight could develop easily if personalities are so inclined. When you sit by another because there's no other place, you signal an apology with a smile and lowered eyes, or you apologize verbally.

When I first became interested in body language, a college professor suggested I try a little experiment with invasion of territory. She suggested that I gradually move in on someone the next time I ate in a restaurant. My husband and I went to dinner with a long-time friend. The atmosphere was intimate, the table small. I quietly slid my entire table setting toward my friend. Then I moved my water and wine glasses. He pretended not to notice at first. Then he blinked more than usual. As I leaned toward him, he abruptly moved his chair a few inches. Conversation became a bit tense. He finally said, "Hey, what's going on here?" I explained that I wanted to see how he acted when someone intruded into his space zone without an invitation.

Police use similar tactics when questioning a suspect. By moving in on a person, they break down his self-assurance. When territory is invaded, even though he may not be conscious of what has happened, his resistance drops.

Americans do not like to be close enough to feel body heat from another person. Beverly, fifteen, had this to say about an overbearing boy: "I simply can't stand him. I find myself on the elevator with him almost every day, and he makes no attempt to move away. It's like having a warm mountain of jelly against me." Body heat changes with the situation we find ourselves in.

Researcher Hall said that when he was a young man, dancing partners varied in body heat. Some were hotter or colder than average. Sometimes the temperature of the same girl changed as they danced. As he got more interested in heat balance, the young ladies always suggested "the need for some fresh air."

One girl said she could detect temperature changes in the chest of her dancing partner. From this observation, she could reliably tell when to "cool it before things went too far." Another girl confided to Dr. Hall, as he studied our space needs years later, that she could tell the emotional condition of her boyfriend from three to six feet away in the dark by the level of his body heat.

Our thermal space indeed has something to say about our emotions. Body temperatures change in the flush of passion or when we are in a cold sweat. Proxemic researchers say a cold stare or a heated argument are not just figures of speech. We send and receive messages by skin temperatures in various parts of our body. This body heat or cold is then transmitted to others, even without touch. If you run the back of your hand up and down in front of your face, at various distances, you will soon see at what distance heat is transmitted. In times of stress, more heat is often generated, as when we get "hot under the collar."

Personalities

Our space needs are related to our personality type. Many studies have been made to determine how different people react to space invasion. Dr. Robert Sommer in *Personal Space* told about a study carried out by William Leipold for his PhD thesis. Students were interviewed individually in either a stress or a nonstress situation. When the student came into the room, he was given either stress, neutral, or praise instructions. Stress instructions said, "We feel that your course grade is poor and that you have not tried your best. Please take a seat, and Mr. Leipold will be in shortly." Neutral instructions said, "Mr. Leipold is interested in your feelings about the introductory course." The praise instructions told the student that he was doing very well in the course. After the student entered and seated himself, Mr. Leipold came in and recorded where the student sat for the interview. Results showed that students who received praise sat closest. Students under stress sat farthest away. Neutrals sat in between. Introverted and anxious students kept their distance. Extroverts with lower anxiety levels didn't seem to mind being closer.

Dr. Leipold's research confirms what many other psychologists have discovered. Introverts seem to need more space about them, while extroverts have a smaller space bubble.

A recent study showed that males and females react differently to crowding. Men respond negatively when they are overcrowded. They become suspicious, combative. A fight develops easily in a mob where males are under stress of crowding. In contrast, females react positively to crowds. They become friendlier, more at ease with each other. Girls seem to enjoy the camaraderie of closeness.

We mark off our territories in public places sometimes by placing a coat, books, or a briefcase on a chair. The object reserves the place for us in our absence. Our neighbors help defend our territory also, up to a point. A study of the good-neighbor effect was done in a college library. As long as the room was not too crowded, and the person was not gone from his seat too long, his neighbor told others, "Yes, the seat is taken." As room density increased, and if the person had been gone almost an hour, then the neighbor gave up the seat.

If we sit in the same chair every afternoon with our friends at a pizza parlor or soda fountain, we expect that chair to be vacant for us. A study of this attitude was made at a campus soda fountain. Ann Gibbs, who conducted the study, approached people sitting at a table. She said, "Excuse me, but you are sitting in my chair." Students who had been seated only a short time did not feel any right to the chair. They moved away. One student who had been sitting only a short time seemed annoyed. Yet he said, "Oh, all right, I'll move." He did not question Miss Gibbs, even though there were many vacant tables around. Students who had been seated a long time strongly resisted the invasion. One fellow who had sat there for twenty-five minutes said, "No, I don't think so," and he refused to move.

We see young adults in a family react this way when someone sits at their place at the kitchen table. In one family where breakfast is not always eaten together, this scene happens often. Mark, fifteen, enters the kitchen. Mark sees his brother Tim sitting in what Mark considers his territory, his usual place at dinner. "That's my place. Move over," he demands.

"What difference does it make?" Tim counters.

"This is where *I* sit!" Mark says emphatically.

What happens next depends on how strongly Mark wants to defend his territory—and who is the bigger.

Space and Status

The way we use space around us gives interesting clues to our status. A judge sits above the jury to show his higher status. In many suburbs, minimum lot and house sizes are set to maintain the status of the community. Status symbols say, "I'm a little better than you." One of the most status conscious groups in our country is the military. You can immediately tell a soldier's rank by the stripes, cut of uniform, braid, and medals he wears. Such things perpetuate our status system, even though some symbols are beginning to tumble.

When a teacher or interviewer sits securely behind the desk, he both literally and figuratively keeps his status between you. The atmosphere warms up quite a lot if the teacher comes around from the desk. At a meeting, if the speaker sits around in a circle with the audience, you get an entirely different feeling about him from what you register if he stands above you at a podium.

We have all heard the term *pecking order* applied to the business world. This term comes from the study of behavior among chickens, which establish a hierarchy when they are about twelve weeks old. The most aggressive chickens peck, while the least aggressive are pecked by others. The most aggressive chickens have a wide range of territory. They roam all around, while the least aggressive can only move in a limited part of the yard.

Suppose you are about to enter someone's office. If you knock, then stop just inside the door to carry on your conversation from that distance, this behavior says you are subordinate to the other person. If you walk across the room about halfway to his desk to talk, you are not quite so inferior to him. If you walk directly to the desk to talk, you rank closer to him. Do you stop far enough away, at a respectful distance, to allow this person to dominate you? Or do you stand close to his desk, towering over him, as if to dominate? The next time you find yourself in such circumstances, stop and think a moment which meaning you want to convey. The choice could make a difference in your relationship.

Think for a moment, too, how a small child feels when you tower over him in domineering body language. To develop better rapport with little ones, get down close to their level when you talk. Sit on the floor. Crouch down low. They'll like you better if you don't seem to be such a giant!

The amount of space around us is one key to status, dominance, and leadership. How we handle space, where we position ourselves at a table in the cafeteria when we are with a group tells what we consider our spatial place, our role in society. Leaders tend to select the head seat when the table is rectangular. Others sit where they can see and make eye contact with the leader.

Where do you sit in a classroom? Many teachers agree that the most interested students sit in the front rows, and the ones more interested in a quick getaway choose aisle seats. Front-row students commonly participate more in discussions. The ones who sit around the wall rank next in participation. They also have an unobstructed view of the teacher. Students who sit in the rear are usually inattentive, more interested in fooling around. Students label their peers who gather in the rear as "goof-offs."

Straight-row arrangement of seats makes discussion more difficult in the classroom. It also gives students the feeling of being on an assembly line. Whether these theories are correct or not, researchers feel that classroom space is divided into zones in which people with similar attitudes and behavior sit together. They also feel that a teacher can learn about the student and his self-image from noting where he chooses to sit.

According to Dr. Hall, each of us has a number of learned "situational personalities." They are the way we respond to intimate, personal, social, and public happenings. He feels that some of us never learn to develop the public phase of our personality. Such people make poor speakers in public places. Others of us have trouble with our intimate and personal zones, a fact well known to many psychiatrists. Some of us cannot endure closeness or crowding. We sense people around us as close or distant. But we seldom know why we consider them this way. Is it because of voice, tone, stance—or distance, the actual air space between us?

Many different things happen at once in communications. We sort out a lot of information before we decide how we feel about something or someone. Our use of space around us is but one factor, a "hidden dimension." This dimension can be extremely helpful in understanding personalities, if we bring a new awareness to it.

CHAPTER NINE

Body Language Spoken Here

I did not even quite know the language.
JAMES MATTHEW BARRIE

Just as spoken languages differ from country to country, so does the language of posture and gesture. Visitors to foreign countries might well remember the comments of anthropologist Dr. Edward Hall, an expert in the field of communications without words. He says, "Watch where people stand when they talk to you, and don't back up if they stand too close. You will feel funny doing this, but it's amazing the difference it makes in people's attitudes."

Many stumbling blocks exist to human understanding. Body language is no exception. Paul, seventeen, described a foreign student whom he had met recently. "He stood so close my eyeballs hurt. After a while I couldn't even follow what he said." Like Paul, many of us find our trend of thought completely lost when some silent message disturbs us. In this case the silent message concerned the space needs of his new acquaintance. To compound matters, the foreign student probably thought Paul was an unfriendly, cold person.

Scientists who have studied proxemics (how we use space around us) say that we miscommunicate with people of other countries especially in this facet of body language. We think, by their need to stand close, that they are pushy and aggressive. They think we are cold and standoffish. Dr. Hall described a meeting with a Polish colleague. Conversation began at close range, too close for Hall. He moved back a few steps. The Pole closed the distance gap. Again Hall stepped away. Now he noticed his friend puzzle over his antics, as if to say, "What have I done to offend you?" The man's thoughts seemed less organized. Hall then realized his colleague's need to stand closer. He says he has actually seen people back the entire length of a corridor to move away from some one whose space needs differ from theirs.

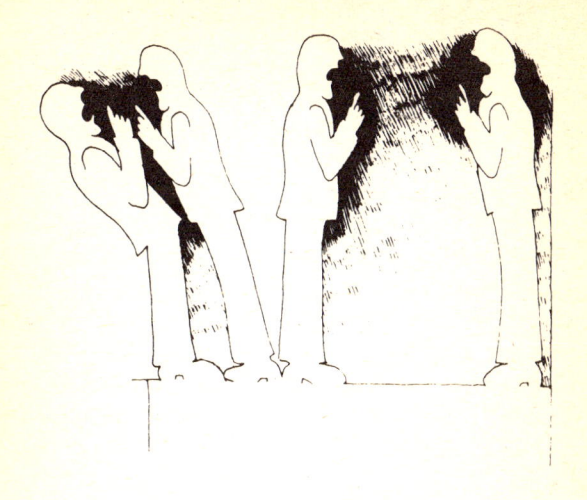

In the United States we normally stand about two to three feet apart in conversation. Unacquainted adults prefer to keep each other at about arm's length, three or more feet apart. Americans are decidedly uncomfortable when someone intrudes into their personal space bubble. In fact, Dr. Hall says that "much of the physical discomfort that Americans experience when foreigners are inappropriately inside the intimate sphere is expressed as a distortion of the visual system." When someone stands close we actually lose sharp visual focus. We may get the feeling of being cross-eyed from looking at something too close. At this range, body heat and breath odor are easily noticed, and most Americans are trained to turn away or direct breath odor away from someone's face.

Dr. Albert Scheflen has studied closely American communication through body postures. He feels that "there are no more than about thirty traditional American gestures," although not all Americans behave exactly alike. A twenty-five-year-old engineer from New England will have gestures different from those of a Midwestern career girl. Still, even an untrained observer will quickly notice certain gestures are characteristic of the culture.

The Arabs

Latin and South Americans, Poles and Italians, as well as Arabs stand close together when they talk. An Arab likes to smell his friend's breath and body odor. An Arab intermediary might ask to "smell the girl" before he arranges a marriage. She may have the smell of anger or discontent. An Arab feels that a person exists somewhere down inside the body and that breath is related to emotions and health. The Arab might comment to a friend, "Your stomach and breath smell bad. Don't stand close in your business today."

Arab cities are extremely crowded. Cities are noisy places, teeming with life, where people touch hands and bodies often. Arabs mutually bathe in breath as they talk, while piercing eyes seem to look right through each other. This exposure pushes the senses to a level that would be unbearable to most Europeans and Americans. Often when an Arab visits the United States, he will long for home where there is human warmth and sensory contact. In Arab homes, no partitions wall off rooms. An Arab does not mind being crowded by people, but he doesn't want to be stifled by walls. To Arabs, to be alone is to stop talking. When they want privacy, they will withdraw to their own thoughts.

Thus, an Arab exchange student who stayed with a Kansas family failed to take the hint that they were uncomfortable when they stopped talking to him easily. He merely assumed they were engaging in a time of privacy. Not until they tried to send him back to exchange program headquarters in Washington, DC, did he realize that something was wrong.

Pushing and shoving in a public place is a common thing in the Middle East. Arabs feel that they have a perfect right to try to force someone to leave if they wish to occupy a particular spot. To an Arab, a public area means anyone has a right to it. They have little concept of privacy outside of their own body.

Our way of polite conversation, in eye movement as well as in body positioning, communicates shame to an Arab. They do not want to walk while talking to you, seeing you only out of the corner of the eye. They want to face you. For an Arab, diplomacy is not only eyeball to eyeball, but breath to breath. To deny a friend your breath is to be ashamed! As Hall explains, in comment on our habit of turning our breath away from others, "Who would expect that when our highest diplomats are putting on their best manners, they are also communicating shame?" An Arab considers himself polite not to look deeply into your eyes as he talks to you. This intensity disturbs us. We may take this eye behavior as a challenge or even as a sexual assault.

When we display our need to stand about four to seven feet apart, an Arab thinks we are unfriendly. Yet Arabs do not always have conversation at very close range. On important social occasions, they may sit across a room to talk.

In the English-speaking world, we use our hands to accompany our talk relatively little. For Arabs of all social levels, though, gestures are indispensable. One anthropologist recently put together a dictionary of Arab gestures. He found specific definitions for 247 motions. Some Arab gestures are similar to those of an American. Others are quite opposite.

When Arabs shake their head from side to side, this gesture means *yes* instead of *no*. To say *no* nonverbally, Arabs move their head upward and slightly click the tongue. Can you imagine trying to bargain in an Arab marketplace without knowing this body language?

Arab gestures often send useful and respectable information although many of them would be considered obscene in other cultures, an anthropologist reports. In Saudi Arabia, when a man kisses the top of another man's head, he is making an apology. In at least four Arab countries, people flick their right thumbnail against their front teeth to show they have little or no money. Some Arabs touch their nose three times to show friendship. Arab gestures are always made with the right hand, not the "unclean" left hand.

As you can see, communications can fall apart readily with such differences in body language. We may easily misinterpret the emotions and meaning intended in a situation.

Jennie, traveling abroad last summer, discovered great differences in body language. She recalled with embarrassment that an Arab family they met noticed how her father backed away. When they walked along the street, they often saw Arabs stare at them, since this eye behavior is not considered impolite. "I had the uneasy feeling that something must be unbuttoned," she said with a laugh.

The Spanish

In Spain Jennie watched two men along the street, arms linked at nearly armpit level. They talked animatedly, breathing into each other's faces. Along the Mediterranean, teen-age Spanish girls often enjoy the *paseo,* or evening stroll, arm in arm or holding hands with each other. Both are examples of perfectly acceptable street behavior that might very well be greeted with raised eyebrows here.

Habits of queuing up differ in many countries, and Spain was no exception. In church, Jennie watched people mill around. They all made their way to the communion rail from every section of the church at once, without the sense of orderliness of lining up, row by row, that we prefer. At a bullfight in Malaga, as at events in many European towns, she found that people did not line up to buy tickets. Instead, they pushed and shoved, as hands waved money at the cashier. Everyone edged their way into any public event.

In the United States, most people regardless of wealth or status are served on a first-come first-served basis. In Europe, where remnants of the class system still exist, many feel group conformity offends their individual dignity. One Pole claimed that "Americans queue up like sheep."

Eye movements vary from one culture to another. Our normal eye contacts last about one second before someone looks away. We listen in conversation with our neck slightly outstretched. We nod attentively or murmur, "um, uh, huh," as our eyes look at the other person.

Spanish-American males greet each other in a stereotyped embrace. First, they place their head over the other's right shoulder and give three little pats on the back; then the head goes over the left shoulder with three more quick pats.

The English

In England, Jennie found a fixed stare and an occasional eye blink were normal attentive-listener patterns. Unaccustomed to this response, Jennie at first thought her English friend was bored or just tuned out. Englishmen never seem to know for sure if we are listening, while we wonder if they understand us at all.

Englishmen have variety in their eyebrow placement, according to one kinesic researcher. Some look perpetually surprised to Americans, with extremely high brow position. Others, usually of lower socioeconomic level, look almost beetle-browed in their low placement.

The English are definitely a noncontact people. A well-bred person there would never touch someone else without his consent. Even a brother or sister apologize for the slightest accidental contact. According to Dr. Montagu, touching has been culturally defined as vulgar by the English.

A nurse cares for a baby in England. Then a governess takes over at an early age. Public demonstrations of affection are also considered vulgar by most English people.

English children are conditioned early to sharing space. They have probably been brought up in a shared nursery, although the oldest child in the family may have a room alone until she goes away to school. Americans are more accustomed to having a room alone or at least a part of one. Americans who work in England expect to have an office or an enclosed space in which to work. We prefer to have a door to close if we choose. The English seem puzzled by this need.

Englishmen and Europeans cross their legs differently from American men, with one leg crossed over another, in a manner that may appear effeminate to us. Men in the United States tend to cross their legs in a figure-four pattern. One leg is horizontal with the ankle resting on the other knee. Young boys pick up this totally American gesture at a very early age. Girls sometimes cross their legs this way, too, when they are wearing slacks or jeans.

The Germans

If the English and Americans seem incompatible in their body language, the Germans and the Americans are even further apart. Germans go to extremes to preserve their private space sphere. Dr. Hall, one of our foremost researchers in space needs, says he was once called in for advice. He was asked, "How do you get Germans to keep doors open?" A door is taken most seriously by Germans. They consider open doors sloppy and disorderly.

An American student in Germany said she "found

the doors superheavy, double, and probably soundproof. They seem to truly protect people." Closed-door business patterns sometimes cause friction between Germans and Americans, since we are more casual about such things. Americans tend to think that closed doors indicate something sinister, like a conspiracy, going on. Germans feel open doors are too relaxed, not businesslike.

Germans are also rigid compared to many other cultures in their tactile needs. They feel even less need to touch or embrace than the English. Their culture emphasizes the unbending warrior. The father dominates, and the others in the family are subordinate to him. The space bubble surrounding a native of Germany is indeed a large one. If you come within seven feet of most Germans, they will feel that you have intruded upon them. Americans like to move their chairs about to adjust to a meeting or situation. In contrast, Germans consider that changing the position of one's chair is a violation of mores. One German newspaper editor who came to the United States had his visitor's chair bolted to the floor at a "proper distance." He simply couldn't tolerate the American habit of always adjusting the chair in his office.

The French and the Austrians

At the other end of the tactile scale, the French love to be in touch with people. In their crowded living quarters, and in the layout of their cities, everything is designed to keep sensory involvement in high gear. Small sidewalk cafes with many tables close together typify the cities and towns of France. When a Frenchman talks to you, you know very well that he is looking at you. American girls who spent a summer in France complained that they felt almost deprived when they returned to their country. A Frenchman enjoys looking at attractive females, and he does so quite openly. In the United States males are much less obvious in their girl watching. When Frenchmen line up to wait for the Metro (subway), they lean and press on each other, crowd around, and feel no need to apologize for body contact. Dr. Montagu says Americans line up for a bus like "sparrows on a telephone wire."

A Frenchman who traveled in the United States was amazed at our "docile" restaurant habits. "You line up to be seated, and you accept any table offered," he observed.

At a party, a Frenchman will greet the host and most of the guests (ladies included) with a handclasp. He may kiss the ladies' hands. He again goes through this routine when he leaves the party.

At a party last summer I met an Austrian medical student and his wife who were in the United States for three months on a church exchange program. When I shook hands with both Herb and Belita, they remarked that they had seen very few American women shake hands when they were introduced. In Austria, though, women always extend their hand in greeting, they told me. Austrians are not nearly as rigid in their space needs as their neighboring Germans.

Americans in the past ten years have evidenced a "need to touch" too. My friend Dottie commented that when she had something important to say, something that might risk losing a friendship or upset her friend, she would always go in person rather than telephone. She said, "I feel more in touch. I like to be able to actually touch my friend. On the phone only the words come through. Too often misunderstandings happen this way." Dottie went on to explain, "All of my feelings, including the nonverbal part of the message, are so important to what I'm saying."

The Japanese

The Japanese people find the business methods of Americans sometimes difficult to understand. "You are in such a hurry to make a decision, to come to terms," a young Japanese woman said. In contrast, the Japanese talk around a situation for a long time. They are sensitive to all the nonverbal communications while Americans take great pains to be logical and decisive. As a result, some Japanese find Americans frustrating to deal with.

The tea-drinking ceremony is an important part of decision making to a Japanese. An American said, "The Japanese talk around and around a point and never do get to it."

Japanese mothers spend much time with their babies. They strive for a passive, contented child. American mothers are more verbal and goal-oriented with their babies. In Japan, there is much body contact for children. Whole families bathe collectively until the child is about ten years old. Then a sudden break comes in tactile contact.

A young Catholic priest told this story: "While ice skating in Japan not long ago, a Japanese boy of about high-school age skated up to me and took my hand. I was quite uncomfortable. He began skating around the rink with me. He merely wanted to practice his English. In his culture, a man acting this way at a sporting event would not be considered out of line. I saw children going to school, boys with other young boys, or girls with girls, holding hands."

Like many other Orientals, the Japanese are sometimes thought of as inscrutable. They learn not to show their true emotions. Accordingly, Americans sometimes are bewildered. A Japanese child learns to smile as a social duty, much as he is taught to bow. He must show happiness, so he won't bring pain or sorrow to his friends. One researcher told of an extreme example: A young woman servant smilingly asked for permission to go to her husband's funeral. She returned later in the day with his ashes in a vase. Actually laughing, she said, "Here is my husband." Her Western-world employer found her heroic facial expression difficult to fathom.

If you ask a negative question of a Japanese, the answer may confuse you. For example, we might ask, "Isn't it raining outside?" If it is, we would answer, "Yes." They would say, "No (shaking their head), it is raining." For this reason, we often think they respond with opposite head gestures to our yes/no head gestures.

Emy Bruce, a gracious young Japanese language specialist for a scientific community in the State of Washington, explained some head gestures of her people. "Japanese nod their heads very often in conversation. Sometimes they are agreeing. They take great pains to make a person feel his words are welcome. They respect a speaker's point of view." Mrs. Bruce interprets for scientists visiting from Japan. She recalled noticing a common posture trait of these visitors. "The posture is very humble, shoulders bowed forward, head slightly bent." Japanese also bow in greeting or to recognize a superior. Status is well defined in Japan.

Eye gestures of the Japanese are similar to those of an American. Blinking is not considered a proper response to a companion. The Japanese also frown on rolling eyes upward or looking out of the corner of the eye. That behavior would be considered furtive.

Although the Japanese have relatively few hand gestures, there is one typical of men in an informal setting. When a man makes a small goof, he scratches his head, as if to say, "What should I do?" In familiar surroundings, males respond this way often.

Japanese females often cover their mouth the entire time they are talking. A Japanese girl is not supposed to show you her entire mouth full of teeth. She will commonly keep her hand in front of her mouth when she laughs, in respect for her listener's comfort. Mouth juices may also spit out at you when certain words are pronounced.

If a Japanese student comes to an American home, she may laugh or smile a lot, to the point that Americans may wonder what's so funny.

Japanese children are taught to choose a happy conversational subject. They learn very early not to gripe to a friend. Generally Japanese are an extremely subdued people. They stand and sit very still, with hands at rest. They speak softly and do not raise their voice, even to scold children. Japanese were shocked when American military personnel spanked their children. To the Japanese, such a loss of self-control or show of anger is a great shame.

Kissing in the Orient is a private act of love play. Public kissing embarrasses or arouses disgust. Japanese look away if they see a visitor display this behavior. For this reason, the love scenes in American movies are censored out when they are shown in Japan.

Japanese do not kiss their children, although they may pat the head or hug a child when he is very small. When a husband leaves for work, he bows to his wife, and she to him, with no physical contact. when he returns, the greeting is much the same.

A Japanese student would be horrified if a boy put his arm around her waist or on her shoulder on a first date — or on the fifth date! This conduct is considered too familiar.

Some other taboos in Japanese culture include whistling at someone or clicking the fingers or tongue in disgust.

The homes and gardens in Japan further reflect their serene nature. The Japanese have a very beautiful way of using spaces. They firmly believe that memory and imagination should be part of our knowledge. Therefore, one of the rocks in a Japanese garden is always hidden. They purposely lead you to a spot where you can discover something for yourself.

Chileans and Other Cultures

We sometimes group Mexicans and South Americans together. In fact, they are much different in their culture. The Spanish in South America are a proud people. They look you right in the eye, not in defiance, but in respect as an equal. Mexicans are generally a humble people and lower their eyes frequently.

In Chile, young girls or women always take their

mother's arm when they go out shopping. They may link arms, or they may take the older woman's elbow, much as we would do if the woman actually needed physical help on the street.

Chileans show their tremendous love for children in many ways. My friend Maria-Ines told this story: "When we go into a store with a baby, everyone has to hold the child, even though they are strangers. They pass him around, and everybody comments, 'What a beautiful baby.'" Her American husband was surprised at the attention lavished on babies and small children. Chileans also pat children on the head to show affection.

A common Chilean gesture used in familiar surroundings is made by bunching fingers and the thumb close together, then raising them to the lips with a kissing sound, as the fingers stretch outward in a movement that says, "It was *magnifico*!" Maria-Ines explains that your favorite cousin might respond this way when you have served a beautiful dinner.

Both males and females use this gesture with people they know well. It is not appropriate in a formal situation.

In Chile, as in many foreign countries, whistling at a football game or public event is impolite. We cheer and whistle when we like something. There, to whistle is considered rude, a sign of extreme disapproval. It is equivalent to our booing a performer.

Some body gestures are conscious and have a readily understood meaning to people of that culture. Males in most cultures respond to a pretty girl, but each in their own way. When an Italian sees a pretty girl, he signals appreciation by pulling on his ear lobes. An Arab strokes his beard or chin. In Libya, men twist the tips of their forefingers into their cheeks when they speak to beautiful women. Some Arabs blow smoke in a girl's face to show they desire her. Englishmen strike an extremely casual posture and look away. An American follows the female with his eyes and shows a slight smile. His eyebrows may raise upward, and he may say, "Hmm, not bad," as he appraises the view. A Japanese carefully conceals his interest, never turning around and letting his eyes follow a girl's movements.

Some gestures are easily understood in many cultures. The hitch-hiker's thumb extended is one. Outstretched arms and open palms are also considered almost universal motions. They show a desire for peace, or they extend an inviation to comfort.

One of the unique features of American communications is that we have very few technical and formal rules. Yet we are quite burdened with many informal restrictions. Americans as a whole are inhibited since we don't clearly know what the rules are. We can only say when they have been violated.

For example, you might say, "I don't know specifically how far away you should stand. But I do know when you've come too close for comfort. Or I know very well when you've used body language that's out of place for the circumstances."

Most of us are only dimly aware of our silent language. Yet we use it every day. We can see how, in spite of similarities on the surface, we are quite different from other cultures in our body movements. As Dr. Hall once noted, Americans who represent our country abroad should be schooled in nonverbal communications as well as the spoken language.

Scientists feel that someday we will learn to "communicate on purpose" with our total message. The study of communication beyond words is a young science. Yet amazing things have been discovered. We have begun to see how words twist and turn in our silent language. We have become aware of ourselves as multi-sensory human beings, communicating on many different levels in the same instant. The sense of touch and the use of space around us have become tools in the communication process.

We begin to ask questions of ourselves. Do we choose the safe, secure seat at a party, with friends we already know? Or do we take a chance and seek out a new acquaintance, a choice that could be a more mature one? Do we offend others by our superior mannerisms? What message does our body send when we enter a group?

The image we have of ourselves is rapidly transmitted in our body language. The image we believe of ourselves, says Dr. Robert Sommer, "becomes a self-fulfilling prophecy." Yet few of us are truly aware of the message we send. Communications fly fast and furiously via body language. Some of us are more attuned to the messages than others.

Perhaps now you may begin to read the body language of those around you more clearly. You may also better understand your own silent language. You might be surprised to learn what others see!

Selected References

Birdwhistell, Ray L. *Introduction to Kinesics*. Louisville: University of Louisville Press, 1952.

Feldman, Sandor. *Mannerisms of Speech and Gestures in Everyday Life*. New York City: International University Press, 1969.

Goffman, Erving. *Behavior in Public Places*. New York City: The Free Press, 1963.

────── *Interaction Ritual*. Garden City, N.Y.: Anchor Books, 1967.

────── *Presentation of Self in Everyday Life*. Garden City, N.Y.: Anchor Books, 1959.

────── *Relations in Public*. New York City: Basic Books, Inc., 1971.

Gordon, Calvin W. *The Social System of the High School*. Chicago: The Free Press of Glencoe, 1957.

Hall, Edward T. *The Hidden Dimension*. Garden City, N.Y.: Doubleday, 1966.

Lowen, Alexander. *Physical Dynamics of Character Structure*. New York City: Grune and Stratton, Inc., 1958.

Montagu, Ashley. *Touching, the Human Significance of the Skin*. New York City: Columbia University Press, 1971.

Morris, Desmond. *The Naked Ape*. New York City: McGraw-Hill, 1967.

Scheflen, Albert E. "Human Communication," *Behavioral Science*, Vol. 13, 1968.

──────── "Significance of Posture in Communications Systems," *Psychiatry*, Vol. 27, No. 4, Nov. 1964.

──────── "Quasi-Courtship Behavior in Psychotherapy," *Psychiatry*, Vol. 28, 1965.

Sommer, Robert. *Personal Space: the Behavioral Basis of Design*. Englewood Cliffs, N.J.: Prentice-Hall, 1969.